Dixie Limited

Dixie Limited

*Railroads, Culture,
and the Southern Renaissance*

Joseph R. Millichap

THE UNIVERSITY PRESS OF KENTUCKY

Publication of this volume was made possible in part by a grant
from the National Endowment for the Humanities.

Copyright © 2002 by The University Press of Kentucky

Scholarly publisher for the Commonwealth,
serving Bellarmine University, Berea College, Centre
College of Kentucky, Eastern Kentucky University,
The Filson Historical Society, Georgetown College,
Kentucky Historical Society, Kentucky State University,
Morehead State University, Murray State University,
Northern Kentucky University, Transylvania University,
University of Kentucky, University of Louisville,
and Western Kentucky University.

Editorial and Sales Offices: The University Press of Kentucky
663 South Limestone Street, Lexington, Kentucky 40508-4008

02 03 04 05 06   5 4 3 2 1

Library of Congress Cataloging-in-Publication Data

Millichap, Joseph R.
Dixie Limited : railroads, culture, and the southern renaissance /
Joe Millichap.
p. cm.
Includes bibliographical references (p.) and index.
ISBN 0-8131-2234-1 (cloth : alk. paper)
1. American literature—Southern States—History and criticism. 2. American
literature—20th century—History and criticism. 3. Southern States—
Civilization—1865- 4. Southern States—In literature. 5. Railroads—
Southern States. 6. Railroads in literature. I. Title.
PS261 .M45 2002
810.9'975—dc21   2001004661

Contents

Preface

The thunder of the great flanged wheels, the long retreating
wail of the whistle.

Thomas Wolfe, *The Face of a Nation*

A study essaying topics as powerful and pervasive, as considerable and complex as railroads, culture, and the Southern Renaissance requires some explanation, justification, and qualification.
My first chapter will serve as a more formal introduction defin-
ing the materials and methods, as well as the contexts and texts
that will comprise the body of this work. These prefatory remarks
will provide a less formal discussion of backgrounds and intentions, as well as traditional acknowledgments and obligations.

The present study combines long-term personal and professional interests. Railroads have always been an individual pur-
suit, beginning with boyhood trips to the long vanished Union
Station of my hometown in the company of my father and grandfather. In both teaching and writing, my scholarly research and
publication has focused on twentieth-century American literature, in particular the fiction of the modern South. Recent cultural criticism suggested new ways to combine my avocation and
vocation in a contextual reading of railroads and culture in the
literature of the Southern Renaissance.

However, no specific program of cultural or literary theories
determines the development of the present study. My scholarship has complemented my teaching, so it has been more practical than theoretical in both method and manner. I was trained in
traditional American and Southern studies, with their emphasis
on literary appreciation, close analysis of texts, interpretation

within interdisciplinary contexts, and evaluation in terms of national and regional concerns. Contemporary critical formulations of intertextuality, canonicity, and cultural meaning in terms of gender, race, and class have influenced my thinking as well—especially in the cultural formation, reception, and interpretation of complex technologies such as railroads.

At the same time, my reading of railroads and the Southern Renaissance is written somewhat in response to recent revisionist criticism of Southern culture and literature. Such revision forms part of the natural progression in any discipline: a thorough reconsideration of formulations, histories, and canons in the Southern Renaissance has helped overcome the inherent stasis in traditional Southern studies. Still, the agendas, methodologies, conclusions, and implications in recent revisionist criticism require better dialogue with traditional approaches. At times, some recent revisionism seems as driven by political correctness and academic politics as the more rigid traditional readings of the development of Southern culture, the canon of Southern literature, and the formulation of the Southern Renaissance.

I have not attempted, however, either a theoretical or a comprehensive work on the formulation, history, and canon of the Southern Renaissance. My cultural reading of railroads in some of their important contexts and texts simply reaffirms some aspects of traditional approaches to these topics and suggests possibilities for critical dialogue. To put it very plainly, my study of Southern railroads, culture, and literature confirms that something like a "Renaissance" can be discerned in the South between the two world wars, that this development was occasioned by the tensions and conflicts between tradition and change in "Dixie," and that these developments focused the writing of both canonical and neocanonical figures in the region throughout the twentieth century. This is not to deny that the Southern Renaissance is a cultural construct, that many other changing aspects of modern culture influenced these literary contexts and texts, or that the changes in the South were necessary and salutary.

My primary purpose in the present study is suggested by my title—a reading of the complex, often ambivalent relation and resonance among technology, culture, and literature as represented by railroads in selected writers and works of the South-ern Renaissance, very broadly defined. To the extent my study accomplishes its purposes, credit must be given to those who pro-vided assistance and support over its lengthy evolution. My first obligation is to the many writers and thinkers, scholars and crit-ics who influenced my appreciation, analysis, interpretation, and evaluation of Southern letters—both those more formally cited below, as well as to those individuals and institutions that have affected me as profoundly, if less formally, over the course of my career.

Next, friends, colleagues, and administrators at Western Kentucky University and other institutions provided encourage-ment, suggestions, and support. My administrative colleagues at Western supported my study by way of time released from teach-ing and other duties and by varied research funding. Departmen-tal colleagues, staff, and both undergraduate and graduate students indulged me in the discussion of railroads, technolo-gies, and American texts.

Finally, my extended family provided the ineffable though vital support necessary to complete a study of this sort, and with my sincere gratitude this work is dedicated to them. My wife, Pat Bradley, deserves my particular thanks for her help at all stages of my study, from inception to completion. I am grateful for her willingness to share her energy and insight, as well as her computer, while she was herself engaged in a parallel aca-demic project.

Chapter One

Railroads, Culture, and the Southern Renaissance

The presence alone of Faulkner in our midst makes a great difference in what the writer can and cannot permit himself to do. Nobody wants his mule and wagon stalled on the same track the Dixie Limited is roaring down.

Flannery O'Connor,
"Some Aspects of the Grotesque in Southern Fiction"

1

Students of the Southern Renaissance will readily recognize my epigraph as Flannery O'Connor's characteristically clever, ironic, and conflicted assessment of the literary landscape in Dixie as she viewed it in an essay published in 1960, at the moment of transition to another, more contemporary cultural construct we now call post-Southernism. Her controlling symbol of the Dixie Limited also supplies my title for this study, as it neatly encapsulates several subjects, images, and ideas addressed here. O'Connor's complicated metaphor resonates beyond her immediate situation to suggest the complex of meanings inherent in the relation of Southern railroads, Southern culture, and Southern literature.

At the most universal level, Flannery O'Connor's heroic metaphor projects the plight of the apprentice writer who must simultaneously emulate and escape the accomplished master. Her imagery captures a universal instance of influence anxiety, where the master's express threatens to demolish the apprentice's rattle-trap as she negotiates this literary grade crossing. Her meanings become specifically Southern in the regional references of her contrasted vehicles. The mule-drawn wagon persisted as a farm-to-market mode of transport into the twentieth-century South, while the transition to the steam-driven locomotive represented the cultural changes that engendered the Southern Renaissance.

Flannery O'Connor's Dixie Limited is both a universal image and an actual train, so it not only invokes the mythic meaning of "Dixie" but also the practical significance of the "Limited." A train was so-called because, in making fewer stops and operating at greater speeds, its passengers were limited to those able to pay higher fares for better service. As a native Georgian, O'Connor simply may have recalled the name of a well-known train that traversed her home state, but then why not the just as popular Dixie Flyer, or the more symbolic Dixie Land, both components of the Dixie Fleet, which ran on the Dixie Line, propelled by the powerful Dixie class steam locomotives (Castner 10–12)? Through the complex suggestions of her metaphor O'Connor both celebrates and delimits William Faulkner's centrality in, importance to, and influence on the literary landscape of Dixie. After all, Southern railroads empowered middle-class white men, for the most part, and Southern culture generally did the same with Southern letters, as O'Connor well knew.

The continuing critical debate on Flannery O'Connor's subjects, Southern letters and William Faulkner, often has reiterated her striking metaphor, positively in general, but sometimes for differing purposes. The most interesting example remains Louis D. Rubin Jr.'s uncharacteristic disremembering in his essay "The Dixie Special: William Faulkner and the Southern Renascence" (1982), which asserts Faulkner's special place within Southern literature by transforming O'Connor's phrase to "nobody likes to get caught on the tracks when the Dixie Special comes through" (40–41). Although few doubted the Mississippi master's special status when O'Connor formulated her vision of the literary South in 1960, many were questioning it over the next decades, especially after Richard King's interrogating study, *A Southern Renaissance: The Cultural Awakening of the American South, 1930–1955* (1980), which reads the historical narrative of the Southern Renaissance as a Freudian family romance. When Rubin delivered his belligerent defense of the critical/historical status quo at the University of Mississippi's Yoknapatawpha Conference in 1982, on the theme of William Faulkner and the Southern Renaissance, he was addressing Richard King and other doubters.

A less combative presentation of Rubin's position exists in his more introspective essay, "The Boll Weevil, the Iron Horse, and the End of the Line: Thoughts on the South" (1979). Rubin's self-searching touches on all the aspects of the South considered here—Southern railroads, Southern culture, Southern literature, and the Southern Renaissance—in their personal and professional dimensions for him. His title proves both playful and ironic, for the "Boll Weevil" is a branch line gas-electric train, and the "Iron Horse" is a hitching post in the form of a horse's head. The first image comes out of his own youth in low-country South Carolina, while the second derives from the Mississippi Delta youth of Walker Percy's autobiographical "last gentleman," Will Barrett. Both symbols resonate personally and professionally for Rubin in regard to the putative "end of the line" for the traditional South and its literature.

Louis Rubin Jr.'s little train—"in its own way emblematic of something every bit as disruptive, as devastating, as the insect" the low-country people fancied it resembled ("Boll Weevil" 199)—is long gone, of course, by the time he writes the essay, along with "many another artifact of youth and young manhood" (205). Such is also the case with Walker Percy's and Will Barrett's discovery of a similar complex of meanings in an iron horse's head surrounded over time by the live oak's bark. Rubin combines both symbols to posit a line of future growth for the South in the simple image of whites and blacks casually eating lunch together at a refurbished railroad café in the junction town of Hamlet, North Carolina. The importance of Rubin's Boll Weevil is found in this continuity of past, present, and future: "It had been *real,* it had *existed,* and for me the little train was process; identity *in* time, not outside it. . . . It was *in* time that it was able to be what it was for me, *in* its continuity" (222, emphases in original). In other words, trains and tracks, places and events, writers and texts still compel our attention in all their persistence, presence, and power over time. We cannot forget, ignore, or deny their existence because they cannot be made to fit our interpretations of the past, the present, or the future.

In the last two decades, revisionist critics have become suspicious of the Southern Renaissance itself, to some extent because of William Faulkner's perceived centrality to it. For example, in his skeptical and provocative study, *Inventing Southern Literature,* Michael Kreyling, while admitting that Southern literature does exist as "an amalgam of literary history, interpretive traditions, and a canon," judges it as a phenomenon not so much "innate" as "cultural product, or 'artefact'" (ix). If the actual existence of Southern literature seems a doubtful proposition to revisionists, the Southern Renaissance becomes downright dubious. Kreyling's study deftly traces the cultural construction of Southern letters from *I'll Take My Stand* (1930), the initial Fugitive/Agrarian cultural and literary manifesto, to *The History of Southern Literature* (1985), the ultimate traditional reading, written by diverse hands but edited by Rubin. For Kreyling, Southern literature viewed from the traditional prospect of the Southern Renaissance is an "orthodox faith . . . revealed by a constant southern identity" (ix). In revisionist terms, these concepts are conservative cultural constructs privileging traditional ideas, writers, and texts—both creative and critical—in terms of gender, race, and class.

Interestingly enough, *Inventing Southern Literature* employs railroad metaphors to describe both the conservative construction of Southern literature and its own revisionist deconstruction of it. Kreyling denies his study is really "a counternarrative that seeks to dynamite the tracks on which the official narrative runs; rather it is a metanarrative, touching on crucial moments . . . where the official narrative is made or problematically redirected" (ix). His literary history begins with the Fugitive/Agrarians: "[Allen] Tate could see the practical and the myth; in his mind the South ran on both tracks" (15). Later, when he questions Faulkner's traditional place in the literary landscape of the modern South, Kreyling reiterates both O'Connor's Dixie Limited metaphor as well as Rubin's Dixie Special recasting of it. Kreyling's own interrogation of Faulkner notes that "several objects lay on the tracks" (140) before the completion of the flawed final epic, *A Fable* (1950), necessitating "the caboose of an afterthought preface" (143); this contradiction of intentions undercuts Faulkner's reliability as the narrator of a "benediction" (xv) for Southern letters in his Nobel Prize speech.

Ironically then, Michael Kreyling's own railroad imagery informs a more recent text, *Dirt and Desire: Reconstructing Southern Women's Writing,* by Patricia Yaeger, a determinedly feminist reader of Southern women's texts. Yaeger's second chapter is entitled "Dynamiting the Rails: Desegregating Southern Literary Studies," and it begins with a reference to Kreyling's "unevenly achieved" goals (34). Her opening paragraph ends with a direct statement of her purposes: "I'm driven by another animus. I want to dynamite the rails" (34). Yaeger, like Kreyling, sees the "official narrative" of modern Southern letters as an "iron path," and, like Flannery O'Connor, one of her important subjects in *Dirt and Desire,* she believes "the Dixie Limited has been bound" for too long by its ineluctable rails (34). For Yaeger, O'Connor's heroic metaphor embraces not just William Faulkner and the "Faulkner industry" (96–97), but the whole traditional formulation of Southern literary studies (34–35, 55, 60). She asks, "But if these old categories have become the mystic self-certainties that I want to blow up, what can I use for nitroglycerine? And where can I plant it?" (34).

"And where better than the tracks themselves," she answers (35). Yaeger's ever provocative and often rewarding study proves richer and denser than Kreyling's, and it includes a good deal of railroad imagery and symbolism in its analysis of texts by both male and female writers of the modern South—in particular, William Faulkner, Eudora Welty, Zora Neale Hurston, and Flannery O'Connor. My own study will try to defuse some of these "explosives" in the chapters that follow; however, I also would endorse some of her "charges." In particular, Yaeger interrogates the Southern tradition by asking what would happen if we blew up the tracks separating it from the other of gender, race, and class in much the same way the actual tracks often divided a small Southern town like Faulkner's Jefferson (39). Yaeger's interrogative assertions prove appropriate for a study published at the opening of a new century for Southern literature, and her often insightful readings certainly will affect the developing dialogue of Southern letters.

At this juncture we might mention another recent study of Southern letters that asks similar questions about formulations, histories, and canons. Richard Gray's *Southern Aberrations: Writ-*

ers of the American South and the Problems of Regionalism (2000) complements the books by Michael Kreyling and Patricia Yaeger discussed above by affirming similar historical arguments and by considering many of the same writers and texts, but also by reconsidering others from the 1930s and 1940s, like Erskine Caldwell and Jesse Stuart, as well as the 1980s and 1990s, like Harry Crews and Doris Betts. Gray, a British academic whose earlier book, *The Literature of Memory* (1977), was a rather traditional reading of the Southern Renaissance, writes astutely about his subjects, both general and particular, as well as with a good deal less invective and animus than some other revisionists. Perhaps because of his outsider's orientation to these American materials, however, Gray does not really complement my discussion of Southern railroads, Southern culture, and the Southern Renaissance.

The engagement of the train as trope by both authors and critics of the Southern Renaissance seems culturally determined by the dominance of the railroad as an emblem of modernity in the South. The steam locomotive developed as the archetypal machine in the American Garden during the nineteenth century, as Leo Marx has ably demonstrated in his classic formulation (14). In Dixie, this development was postponed to the twentieth century by a complicated set of cultural transitions—the slavery controversy, the Civil War, Reconstruction, and the advent of the New South. If the Southern Renaissance can be defined by tension between the traditional and the modern in technological, cultural, and literary terms, then the railroad metaphor proves particularly resonant here in its combination of the practical and the mythic, as Allen Tate saw the two tracks of the Southern cultural tradition. As a technology that changed culture and by extension literature, the railroad became the very type of modernity.

In my reading, the crucial role of the railroad in relation to the Southern Renaissance can be discovered in its practical and mythic significance to the cultural construction of the modern literary landscape in the South and to the recent deconstruction of that process by revisionist critics like Michael Kreyling and Patricia Yaeger. The power, pervasiveness, and persistence of Southern railroad imagery and symbolism asserts the practical utility of Southern culture, Southern literature, and the Southern Renaissance—both as historical realities and as critical concepts. At the same time, their enduring mythic status as cultural formulations in Southern studies necessitates interrogating their power, pervasiveness, and persistence in the imagery and symbolism of tracks and trains.

Again, no better symbolic representation could be found than Flannery O'Connor's heroic simile. William Faulkner is like the Dixie Limited in several theoretical senses, along with several shadings of practical meaning. Like his iron emblem, the author represents an engine of change in a transitional South; certainly Southern letters would never be the same after the publication of the initial Yoknapatawpha novels in 1929. On the one hand, his focused and forceful narrative drive made Faulkner the prototype of the Southern writer. On the other hand, his very presence in the literary landscape often proved limiting both for his own development and for that of others.

In the course of time the express train, important as it was once, gave way to new modes of transport better suited to the changing region; the great steam locomotives remain in Dixie today, if at all, as monuments to a changing past. Even fewer travelers would take Amtrak trains, nostalgic or not, if they still employed Pullman standard sleepers hauled by coal burning engines. Yet, as Louis Rubin insists of his vanished Boll Weevil, these tracks and trains did once exist within the process of time. To understand the continuity of Southern culture, William Faulkner's power and presence must be acknowledged, along with the traditions of writing and reading he represents for Dixie—even at our end of the cultural line extending from the Southern Renaissance to the present.

2

Parallels in the technological, cultural, and literary histories of the South provide striking examples of the persistence of railroads. For example, a railroad map of America in 1861 represents the complex of causes that cost the Confederacy the Civil War. While the Northern states were stitched together in a web of iron, the Southern states were rather loosely knit, with some rail lines still unconnected to any other (Nelson 15). Although the North had over twice the rail mileage of the South, this statistic reveals only half the actual disparity, as the Yankee railroads were better planned, constructed, equipped, and operated. The South also depended on the North for most railroad materials, and it had no ready way to replace them once it was embargoed and blockaded. The Northern strategists' more timely recognition that this war would be the first decided by railroads was balanced only by daring Rebel tactics, prolonging the conflict over four exhausting years until 1865 (Nelson 27–45).

That antebellum railroad map also reveals a complex of attitudes toward trains that gave them special meaning in Southern culture both before and after the pivotal conflict. Although some railroads of the Old South were among the first in the country, they were less quickly or extensively developed than in the North (Stover, *American Railroads* 13–14). Many causes contributed to this deficiency, particularly a profound cultural ambivalence toward technology, industry, and urban mobility. The plantation economy, once established, depended on stability, such that the dynamic expansion of Yankee railroads, factories, and cities seemed its antithesis. Dixie wanted only enough of these new technologies to complement, but not disturb, its cultural status quo. Many of the Old South's rail lines linked inland plantations and towns to coastal and river ports, for the most part oriented east/west rather than north/south, often with little consideration of coordination among lines, which operated on tracks of varied sizes using equipment that could not be easily interchanged (Stover, *American Railroads* 51–52).

The relation of Southern railroads to Southern literature closely follows this outline of the region's cultural ambivalence, so few literary tracks or trains are discovered in antebellum Southern letters. Certainly nothing in the works of the region's writers during the prewar period compares to the complex theoretical considerations provided by Ralph Waldo Emerson, the close observations and practical concerns of Henry David Thoreau, and the romantic recreations of Walt Whitman, or to the ambivalent symbolism of James Fenimore Cooper, Nathaniel Hawthorne, and Herman Melville. By contrast, Edgar Allan Poe, the one major author of the antebellum South, never mentions a railroad, while his closest contemporaries William Gilmore Simms, William

Pendleton Kennedy, and Henry Timrod, have little awareness of this burgeoning technology in their romantic concerns with soul and self, with nature and landscape, with romance and chivalry, and with the plantation and slavery. The same neglect of the new modes in communication, transportation, and production also proved true for the popular genres of sentimental romance and tall-tale humor in the South.

Contemporary revisionists of Southern literary history, such as Michael Kreyling and Patricia Yaeger, complain correctly that the Southern nineteenth century is obscured and/or undervalued in order to draw a sharper contrast with the putative brilliance of the Southern Renaissance. In the case of women and/or African American writers this charge is true, at least to some extent. The women who observed the South in memoirs and novels, like Fanny Kemble and Mary Chestnut, or Harriet Jacobs and E.D.E.N. Southworth, are more aware of the cultural changes around them than their white male contemporaries. Slave narratives are perforce more observant of the contemporary landscape as well. Indeed, the metaphorical structuring of the Underground Railroad pays homage to the new technology as the engine of change for the entire American culture in the nineteenth century. The most notable example is Frederick Douglass's autobiographical *Narrative* (1845), in which he buys a railroad ticket to leave Baltimore for Boston, in a south-north journey confirming slaveholders' fears of easy rail connections.

Southern ambivalence about technology not only lost the Civil War but cost the South much of those transportation, communication, and manufacturing capabilities it had developed (Stover, *Railroads of the South* 58–59). No single image of Yankee destruction remains as powerful in its symbolic shorthand as "Sherman's neckties," rails ripped from roadbeds through the heart of Dixie, heated over pyres of wooden railroad ties, twisted around tree trunks, and left knotted like string cravats. Burned bridges, deserted depots, gutted shops, and dilapidated rolling stock were the postbellum heritage of all Southern rail lines. During Reconstruction, railroad and telegraph lines, as well as factories and foundries, had to be rebuilt, often by former Confederate leaders in collusion with Yankee capitalists to exploit Southern resources, both natural and human (Nelson 50–69).

As new sources of social power, technologies such as trains and textile mills assumed an ambivalent symbolism in the New South, which in turn made them even more culturally significant (Ayers 139). In one sense, the New South was created by completing the railroad map of the Old South, and new cities and industries burgeoned where new rail lines met or crossed existing ones. For the first time, the new Southern railroad network also made workable connections with the other sections of the country, even as its new Limiteds perpetuated regional failings such as racial segregation in their accommodations (Stover, *Railroads of the South* 148). Southern raw materials streamed northward, and Northern manufactures flooded southward in a colonial imbalance of commercial and cultural power that extended to literature (Nelson 179–82).

The Civil War, Reconstruction, and the New South, with their increased emphasis on railroads as a force in Southern culture, naturally influenced Southern writing. Of course, realism in itself would have placed more trains on the Dixie scene, as markers of the structural changes transforming the regional culture if nothing else. Again, Southern realists such as Samuel Clemens, the region's only major author of the postbellum period, may not have depicted as many railroads as their northern counterparts, William Dean Howells and Henry James, but they did employ them more symbolically. For Clemens's persona, Mark Twain, the financing of railroads corrupted the times in *The Gilded Age* (1873), the steam locomotive sunk the pastoral steamboat era in *Life on the Mississippi* (1875), and train tracks traced one more important symbolic marker of modern technological and cultural imperialism in *A Connecticut Yankee in King Arthur's Court* (1889). Again, the revisionists' point—that the twentieth-century formulation of the Southern Renaissance neglected the nineteenth—holds true to some extent, but Clemens/Twain, as both person and persona, becomes, much like Poe, a problematic exemplar given the complicated racial dynamics in the works of both writers.

The popular genres that contextualize Twain's masterpieces also revealed more trains; the raucous humor of the Old Southwest rode the rails during Reconstruction, postbellum sentimental romances in the South employed the new mode of transport to fulfill true love, and local-color realism in its Southern varieties considered the comic effects of the railroad in the back country. For example, the traditional folk figure of "The Arkansas Traveler" now is transported by "A Slow Train through Arkansas." William Faulkner's railroad-building forbear, Colonel W.C. Falkner, also constructed romantic novels such as *The White Rose of Memphis* (1881), which concludes with a breathless train race. More realistic fictionist writers—George Washington Cable, Grace King, and Kate Chopin for example—provide better evidence of the "official" neglect by Southern critics asserted by Michael Kreyling, Patricia Yaeger, and other revisionist critics. However, such treatment was so widespread in American literary studies until the last few decades that Southern exemplars were little less neglected than the so-called "regionalists" and "local colorists" in other parts of the nation.

3

The results of the stronger railroad system forged by the New South may be seen in the Golden Age of Southern railroading that followed between the two world wars, an era at least partially responsible for the rise of the Southern Renaissance. All these developments in Dixie mirrored those taking place across the nation. American rail expansion peaked in 1916 at 254,000 route miles, while the nationalization of the railroads from 1917 to 1920 in response to the transportation crises of World War I pushed the number of industry employees to over two million (Stover, *American Railroads* 165–66). Rail mileage and employment dropped during the Depression decade, but passenger and freight volumes would hit new highs with the home-front efforts of World War II, which also saw the beginnings of what would become the Sun Belt South.

Developments in Southern railroading during the 1920s were more marked after a new set of strong regional carriers emerged from corporate consolidations accomplished earlier in the century. The Dixie Line (more formally, the Nashville, Chattanooga, and St. Louis) joined the Southern Railway, the Louisville and Nashville, the Atlantic Coast Line, the Seaboard Airline, and the Illinois Central as practical powers and cultural institutions of almost mythic import. The names of their fast trains fired the imagination of the South, such that the Dixie Limited joined The Crescent Limited, The Pan-American, The Champion, The Orange Blossom Special, The City of New Orleans, and others romanticized in the lyrics of ballads and blues (Beebe and Clegg 200).

The newly important rail network represented the reconciliation, prosperity, and sophistication necessary for a Southern literary flowering, one important enough to become a force on the larger American scene by the end of the 1920s. Cultural considerations traditionally begin with H.L. Mencken's scathing portrait of a benighted South in his infamous essay "The Sahara of the Bozart" (1920), then jump a decade to the publications of 1929, the annus mirabilis during which appeared both William Faulkner's *The Sound and the Fury* and Thomas Wolfe's *Look Homeward, Angel,* as well as a number of lesser works such as Robert Penn Warren's first published book, *John Brown: The Making of a Martyr.* The writers who created these works were born about the turn of the century and came of age during this heyday of Southern railroading. William Faulkner (1897–1962) was the heir of the Mississippi Falkners who made their money building railroads, and his first drawings and stories featured trains (Blotner, *Faulkner* 34). Thomas Wolfe (1900–1935) was the scion of a North Carolina family whose resort home was largely created by railways, and at thirty-four he claimed to have traveled "between 125,000 and 150,000 miles by train" (*Notebooks* 2.79). Robert Penn Warren (1905–1989) was the native son of a town founded by the crossing of regional main lines on the border of Kentucky and Tennessee with a railroad depot where "you could come by the *New Republic* or *Poetry* if you were that ilk of traveler" (*Portrait* 53).

Moreover, these Southern railroads literally engendered the artistic ambivalence discovered in the modernist treatment of traditional materials that characterized the Southern Renaissance, at least in traditional considerations (Gray, *Literature of Memory* 1–9; Singal, *War Within* 3–10; Bryant 1–7). The development of railroads, along with other technologies of the nineteenth century, had influenced twentieth-century modernism; the power and speed of railroads not only affected modernist themes such as the sense of disconnection and alienation in the age of the machine, but they also affected modernist style and its use of fragmentation, juxtaposition, and montage as artistic technique. The landscape, especially the cityscape, was radically reframed by the window of a speeding express. Even in the works influenced by these sophisticated literary practices, Southern writers returned to youthful times and places for their narratives, images, and symbols.

Of course, these divided aspects of the self were mirrored in alienation of the self and other, of the individual and society, of the coterie and the culture. The progenitors of the Southern Renaissance were indeed figures who fit these patterns of personal and professional division. William Faulkner provides the most important and interesting example, as his several biographers have demonstrated. Contemporary Faulkner critics correctly insist that much of his early disaffection from Dixie, like much of the author's later acceptance of the South, consisted of self-fashioned posing in response to cultural expectations. So revisionist readers discern several "Faulkners," created in much the same fashion as his fictional characters.

These self-generated caricatures do exist at both ends of Faulkner's canon and career, from the alienated younger writer of the early sketches to the inspired older author of the Nobel Prize acceptance speech (Watson 1–5). Michael Kreyling questions not just the "Major Figure" of *A Fable* but the fledgling creator of the somewhat autobiographical Quentin Compson. Kreyling observes that Faulkner "had Quentin choose suicide, . . . giving his survivors in the study of the South our central, agonistic, split-personality model" (5). Such interpretations tend to conflate character and creator as well as self and others. An alternate reading of Quentin's suicide might suggest that Faulkner was moving beyond the dead-end of the culture "riven by miscegenation, incest, racial guilt, and shame" (Kreyling 5) in most of his works through the resurrection of Quentin in *Absalom, Absalom!* (1936).

4

Another instance of a resurrected character provides a better example of Faulkner's changing attitudes toward his Yoknapatawpha materials, in this case the problematic other of gender, race, and class as represented in the sexual dimensions of railroad imagery evidenced in *Sanctuary* (1931) and *Requiem for a Nun* (1951). Temple Drake is certainly the symbolic center of *Sanctuary,* but the central observer is Horace Benbow, whose more mundane fate counterpoints the horrors that befall those of its heroine, though both might be considered at least distant cousins to Quentin Compson in literary terms.

At the opening of *Sanctuary,* Horace has left his new home in the Delta and walked at least part of the way to Jefferson along the tracks, stopping to sleep in a boxcar on a siding, though he has wandered far from the railroad when he blunders into the nest of bootleggers near the Old Frenchman Place. Temple Drake begins her fateful descent when she springs from a special train transporting Ole Miss students to a baseball game at State College, meeting one of her several suitors, Gowan Stevens, at the actual station of Taylor, a few miles down the tracks from Oxford. By the third chapter, both Horace and Temple are trapped by the bootleggers under the domination of the notorious Memphis gangster Popeye.

Throughout the novel, Horace is determined in his movements by the railroad schedules of northern Mississippi, as he still does not drive. He rides the passenger accommodation trains from the apocryphal Jefferson to the actual Oxford and Memphis with realistic train changes at the junction of Holly Springs. By contrast, Temple's movements are fixed by others who transport her by car—the feckless Gowan to the fictional Frenchman's Bend and the ruthless Popeye to the actual Memphis. However, Temple figures in some of the most complex psychosexual imagery of railroads in the Faulkner canon. As we might anticipate, these Freudian images configure gender by means of determining symbolism, and, like the overall narrative, they range from folk idiom to modernist complexity. Miss Reba, who keeps Temple in her Memphis "sporting house," describes its functioning to a visiting yokel in railroad terms: "Look here, mister, folks what uses this waiting room has got to get on the train now and then" (*Sanctuary* 166).

In a much more complicated image, Horace imagines Temple's grotesque violation by Popeye after contemplating a photograph of his wife Belle's daughter, Little Belle. "She was bound naked on her back on a flat car moving at speed through a black tunnel, the blackness streaming in rigid threads overhead, a roar of iron wheels in her ear. The car shot bodily from the tunnel in a long upward slant, the darkness overhead now shredded with parallel attenuations of living fire, toward a crescendo like a held breath, an interval in which she would swing faintly and lazily in nothingness filled with pale, myriad points of light" (*Sanctuary* 177). This bizarre modernist imagery represents a complex junction of psychosexual dynamism, which well may represent biographical subtexts here, and cultural energy in historical terms. Horace has just returned to Jefferson by train from his abortive rescue mission to Memphis—physically, emotionally, and psychically exhausted; at some level he connects the iron logic of patriarchal power and sexual determinism working themselves out in Temple's violated body and his own ruined life.

Temple Drake is resurrected as Mrs. Gowan Stevens in *Requiem for a Nun,* observed this time by Gavin Stevens, Gowan's uncle, and, like Horace Benbow, another Faulknerian philosopher/attorney who proves unable to control life in theory or in practice. *Requiem for a Nun* is a strange hybrid narrative—part prose fiction, part poetic drama—that attempts to come to terms with the worst of Yoknapatawpha's patriarchal, misogynist, and racist past by resurrecting two of its most conflicted and most troubling female figures. In addition to Temple Drake, the other character here reprised is Nancy Mannigoe, a tragic black woman, whose ambiguous role adds the determinations of race to those of gender. Yet Faulkner seems to link the two women, to yoke their intertwined personal histories in the dramatic scenes with the regional history depicted in the fictive chapters.

Organized around three physical structures representative of patriarchal power at the levels of state, county, and town—the Mississippi statehouse, the Yoknapatawpha courthouse, and the Jefferson jailhouse—Faulkner's railroad imagery proves striking, in some ways definitive of his purposes in such constructions throughout his earlier canon. For example, his description of Jackson is entitled "The Golden Dome," in reference to the state capitol, and it draws on the railroad history of Mississippi to trace its story. "And still the people and the railroads: the New Orleans and Great Northern down the Pearl River Valley, the Gulf Mobile and Northern northeast. . . . A line to Yazoo City and the upper river towns made of the Great Lakes five suburban ponds; the Gulf and Ship Island opened the south Mississippi lumber boom" (*Requiem* 110–11). Thus one of Colonel Falkner's historical railroad enterprises, the Gulf and Ship Island, is later connected with the fictional Sartoris railroad, as I will develop further in chapter 2.

Faulkner then projects the railroad as the first of several interlocking systems that range from the Federal highway system to the TVA power grid and seem to objectively determine subjective fate in the changing South. "And the railroad was a part of that system covering the South and the East like the veins in an oak leaf and itself mutually adjunctive to other intricate systems covering the rest of the United States, so that you could get on a train in Jefferson now and, by changing and waiting a few times, go anywhere in North America" (*Requiem* 238–39). Of course, segregated facilities still existed when the connecting express trains crossed into Dixie—and sometimes even when crossing out of the South, depending on the carrier involved.

Finally, an extended metaphor of heroic proportions joins the symbolic structure of the Jefferson jail with the power structure of the archetypal railroad as Faulkner compares the superannuated building, surrounded by new ones, to "the track-walker in the tunnel, the thunder of the express mounting behind him, who finds himself opposite a niche or crack exactly his size in the wall's living and impregnable rock, and steps into it, inviolable and secure while destruction roars past and on and away, grooved ineluctably to the spidery rails of its destiny and destination" (*Requiem* 248). Most striking here is the direct equation of the historical determinism of patriarchal structures and systems with the Freudian railroad imagery recalled from *Sanctuary*.

This metaphor references Temple Drake Stevens, who is able to rescue herself in the face of continuing tragedy despite the bewildered representatives of the patriarchy who surround her. The vehicle of the metaphor, however, represents Nancy Mannigoe, imprisoned in this very building and awaiting her doom for the inexplicable killing of the Stevens child she was hired to nurse. This sequel's closing images suggest, in addition to the conflicts of gender, those of race, as the black and white women probe the tragic determinations that have driven them together. Their personal impasse projects the historical tension just before the Civil Rights era, which would create a conflicted response in the life and work of the Nobel Laureate.

5

William Faulkner's fictions are filled with tracks and trains, in particular those works dealing with the somewhat biographical Sartoris/Benbow/Strothers and McCaslin/Edmonds/Beauchamp families, and in many other texts. In some sense, all these works recreate Faulkner's patriarchal great-grandfather, the Old Colonel, who rode with Forrest during the Civil War, built railroads with convict labor during Reconstruction, and published best-selling romances that featured breathless train chases in the New South. Faulkner's changing attitude toward his biographical and autobiographical characters represents an evolving sense of self and other, the individual and society, and the cultural elite and larger culture.

Faulkner's use of railroad images and symbols follows a similar track, as we will discover below in chapters 2 and 4. These chapters are chronologically divided by the two sets of texts focused by their two contrasting Faulknerian extended families— the Sartorises and Benbows and Strothers in *Flags In the Dust/ Sartoris* (1929) and *The Unvanquished* (1938) and the McCaslins and Edmundses and Beauchamps in *Go Down, Moses* (1942). Both chapters thus are placed in juxtaposition to Thomas Wolfe's fictions considered in chapter 3, which in turn represent changing attitudes toward the other in both Wolfe's and Faulkner's earlier and later works, and by extension in the Southern Renaissance in general over the same decades. In turn, Faulkner's later fiction will be compared with Robert Penn Warren's in chapter 5, Eudora Welty's in chapter 6, and Ralph Ellison's in chapter 7, while in chapter 8 Warren's later poetry moves forward toward the contemporary Post-Southernism of Dave Smith in chapter 9.

Chapter 3 demonstrates similar patterns of development in the real and fictive railroads of the other wunderkind of 1929, Thomas Wolfe. This writer's love of railroads is notorious, as we see noted in a letter to a colleague: "I have been riding in the engine cab of the fastest train in America—and I have soaked up the power and the glory until it's oozing out—and I am going to try to get some of that in my new book" (*Letters* 226). His auto-biographical fictions starting with *Look Homeward, Angel,* edited by Maxwell Perkins from the recently republished *O Lost!,* contain some of the longest train rides in serious literature; his second novel, *Of Time and the River* (1935), was originally intended to be set entirely on board a Pullman express, demonstrating both the freedom and determinism symbolized by railroads. As recent scholarship has shown, his posthumous books were shaped as much by his editor, Edward Aswell, as by the author, but Wolfe wrote the wonderful railroad narratives interpolated in these texts. *The Web and the Rock* (1939) and *You Can't Go Home Again* (1940), like many of William Faulkner's later works, show how their creator could indeed go home again in life and in art to discover a new balance of self and other, of individual and society, and of literary and popular culture.

Robert Penn Warren well might stand as the "poster child" for the sense of personal division that drove the early writers and works of the Southern Renaissance. Joseph Blotner's recent biography revealed, for the first time in print, a little-known suicide attempt at Vanderbilt in 1924 (*Warren* 47–52); if not for the fact that Quentin Compson would not appear on the literary scene for another five years, some contemporary critics might accuse young "Red" Warren of imitation and/or posing. Robert Penn Warren recovered to work a lifetime, another sixty-five years filled with important books in every literary genre that redefined himself, his region, and his literary heritage in their creative and critical engagement of the other. In the process Warren became perhaps modern America's greatest person of letters.

Warren's fiction pictures many trains much in the manner of William Faulkner and Thomas Wolfe—especially in *Night Rider* (1939), *All the King's Men* (1946), *The Circus in the Attic* (1947), and *A Place to Come To* (1972)—but his poetry creates even more complex and ambivalent examples, particularly in the ballads and recollections drawn from his memories of growing up in Guthrie, Kentucky, a division point on the regionally powerful Louisville and Nashville Rail Road. Because of his varied accomplishments in the two genres, as well as the long evolution of his career, Warren, like Faulkner, requires two chapters in my study.

Although Faulkner, Wolfe, and Warren are the most obvious examples of serious writing about railroads during the Southern Renaissance, others abound. I have chosen these three figures and their texts as my primary authors not just for the importance of trains in their work, but for their importance to the study of the Southern Renaissance. In particular, my study will try to establish a sense of development in these figures and in the literary movement they came to represent in traditional literary history. As these writers labored to accommodate the other, so too did the literary and critical elites around them open to admit others as well. Michael Kreyling's, Patricia Yaeger's, and other revisionists' understandable reservations in regard to the generally middle-class white male authors and critics who formulated the history and canon of the Southern Renaissance helped restore balances neglected earlier, though we can still recognize the example and encouragement provided to working-class, black, and female writers and critics by Faulkner, Wolfe, Warren, and others in the initial generation of the Southern Renaissance.

Southern women writers generally present fewer trains, though important exceptions to this tendency exist from the nineteenth century to the present. For example, the earlier generation of transitional figures such as Ellen Glasgow and Elizabeth Madox Roberts use railroads in a naturalistic mode much like their Northern and Midwestern counterparts Edith Wharton and Willa Cather. Later women authors as different as Katherine Anne Porter, Caroline Gordon, Margaret Mitchell, and Carson McCullers included the railroad in their serious and popular recreations of a changing Southern culture in literature. Indeed, a writer like McCullers provides a provocative example of a divided consciousness, recalling that which defined the earlier writers of the Southern Renaissance. Her developing female protagonists come to represent the deeply conflicted McCullers herself in their dissociation from traditional home places in family, community, and region. As we would anticipate from her notable characterization of the regional master as the Dixie Limited, Flannery O'Connor was influenced by Faulkner in her symbolic depiction of trains in her fictions such as *Wise Blood* (1952), "The Artificial Nigger" (1955), and others (Yaeger 81).

Eudora Welty depicts the rail lines of the South, in novels like *Delta Wedding* (1946) and nonfiction like *One Writer's Beginnings* (1984), as powerfully, if not quite as compulsively, as her fellow Mississippian, William Faulkner. In this aspect of her work, as well as in so many others, Welty probably exerts the greatest influence on her female peers and protégés. The very title of her best-known novel, *Delta Wedding,* defines the duality of her vision: on the one hand, the harsh reality of the Mississippi Delta, sometimes called "the most Southern place on earth," and, on the other hand, the romantic transformation inherent in the most primal of cultural customs and social institutions. Interestingly, this dichotomy of theme is represented by two real railroads—the trunk line Illinois Central and the branch line Yazoo Delta—imaginatively recreated for thematic purposes in her narrative set in 1923, a significant date when nothing happened yet everything changed according to Welty.

Race, of course, forms the cultural crux of Southern literature, and Southern racial practice defines itself in its relation to Southern railroads. African American writers from the days of the Underground Railroad through the Great Migration of the twentieth century saw the trains of the South as ambivalently situated symbols of both escape and entrapment. In historical terms, factual reporting like Frederick Douglass's *Narrative* (1845) realized the metaphorical intentions of the Underground Railroad during slavery, while fictions like Paul Laurence Dunbar's *The Sport of the Gods* (1902) revealed railroads as the matrices of corrupted labor practices during Reconstruction and Jim Crow compromises in the New South. Jean Toomer's *Cane* (1923), a pioneering work of the Harlem Renaissance, used both Southern and Northern scenes filled with trains to represent the movement of his black, white, and "mulatto" characters between racial and class identities.

Two African American writers who came of age as much with the Southern Renaissance as with the Harlem Renaissance, Zora Neale Hurston and Richard Wright, extend this realistic observation toward an even more compelling symbolism of trains in works like *Jonah's Gourd Vine* (1934) and *Uncle Tom's Children*

(1938). Again, revisionist critics like Michael Kreyling have argued correctly that African American writers could not have accepted fully the limited vision that engendered the Southern Renaissance, and they are right, at least in historical terms. Patricia Yaeger sees more possibilities for racial crossover, especially in terms of railroad imagery. Yet as the literary movement grew and changed, even white thinkers were alerted to the "double consciousness" that critic W.E.B. Du Bois discovered in the very terms "African and American." In regional perspective, what could have been more divisive of the self than to be both African American and Southern, or, as Fats Waller put it, to be so "black and blue"? Langston Hughes represented this ambivalence toward railroads in his fiction and poetry from the Harlem Renaissance to the Civil Rights movement, from the great migrations to the North after World War I to the southern excursions of the ironically named "Freedom Train" after World War II.

Because of his important intertextualities with both William Faulkner and Robert Penn Warren, black novelist Ralph Ellison becomes the subject of my chapter 7. An important narrative and thematic thrust that may be traced throughout Ellison's canon—as well as Faulkner's, Wolfe's, and Warren's—involves the difficult journey toward self-awareness. The motif most often representing new consciousness is the historical movement of African Americans in a modern Middle Passage from south to north, from past to future, and from rural to urban settings, as represented by the railroads that, for better or worse, facilitated their harsh transitions. Ellison's *Invisible Man* (1952) extends the rail journeys of his earlier stories, such as "Boy on a Train" (1937) and "King of the Bingo Game" (1944), to the published fragments of his long-awaited, though never completed, second novel, especially "A Loss of Innocence" (1970) and *Juneteenth* (2000). His two works of nonfiction, *Shadow and Act* (1964) and *Going to the Territory* (1986), collect his thoughtful criticism of African American culture in terms of literature, music, and art, with many references to the importance of railroads.

Class is the other constraint that revisionist critics place on the traditional construction of the Southern Renaissance. As indicated earlier, the cultural coteries and literary cadres that formulated the literary movement between the world wars in

Richmond, New Orleans, Nashville, and Chapel Hill were more middle class than aristocratic. Moreover, they all—male and female, white and black—were interested in theoretical questions of class structure and in the actual lives of working-class people. These tendencies naturally increased in periods of social strife, particularly the 1930s and the 1960s. Even more recent efforts— the poems of Dave Smith, for example—raise questions of class, along with others of poetic mode, the contemporary in Southern letters, and post-Southernism. Smith's important poems on his family's working-class railroad connections are included in *Cumberland Station* (1977) and *The Roundhouse Voices* (1985); his wife's family provides materials for *Toy Trains in the Landlord's House* (1983) and *Southern Crescent* (1992); while both are represented in his new selected poems, *The Wick of Memory* (2000). All of these Southern railroads advance Smith's most pervasive themes: the inexorable movement of time, the unbearable weight of place, and the frightful fragility of self-identity in the face of such forces. For his reformulation of traditional Southern images and themes, as well as for his anxieties of influence in terms of his poetic and personal relationships with Robert Penn Warren, and his concern with questions of class, Dave Smith centers my penultimate chapter.

Scholars of the Southern Renaissance disagreed about how far into the contemporary period it extended even before they came to question its very existence. Lewis Simpson and Fred Hobson make an interesting case for the useful formulation of post-Southernness, a cultural and literary development determined at least partially by its conflicted relation with the traditional cultural and literary icons of Dixie. For example, Flannery O'Connor's mock-heroic trope of the Dixie Limited enabled her to "shoulder some room in the southern literary space dominated by 'Faulkner' and by the critics who had named him the Major Figure" (Kreyling 128). Yet, as we reconsider her trope, the cultural practices and myths that occasioned it call attention to continuities as well as discontinuities with a regional past, as some, like Patricia Yaeger, have noted (53–55).

Has the Southern Renaissance ended, if we can even agree that it ever did exist, or has it reconfigured itself once again and inserted itself into our new millennial era? In any case, contem-

porary Southern, if not post-Southern, writers in all genres—
and of all genders, races, and classes—extend the regional preoc-
cupation with the images and symbols provided by a cultural
reading of Southern railroads. A few examples include, in chro-
nological order: William Styron, *Lie Down in Darkness* (1951);
Harriette Simpson Arnow, *The Dollmaker* (1954); Jesse Stuart,
Huey, the Engineer (1960); Walker Percy, *The Moviegoer* (1961);
Robert Drake, *Amazing Grace* (1965), John Ehle, *The Road* (1967);
Albert Murray, *Train Whistle Guitar* (1974); Cormac McCarthy,
Suttree (1979); Lee Smith, *Oral History* (1983); Fannie Flagg,
Fried Green Tomatoes at the Whistle Stop Café (1987); and Bobbie
Ann Mason, *Feather Crowns* (1993). These disparate examples
suggest the subject of my final chapter—the continuing search for
post-Southern patterns of persistence and change reiterating, re-
jecting, and perhaps reconfiguring the Southern Renaissance.

Chapter Two

William Faulkner's Cultural History

Railroads in the Sartoris Fictions

... a boy's affinity for smoke and fury and thunder and speed.

William Faulkner, *The Unvanquished*

1

When Flannery O'Connor defined William Faulkner in relation to Southern writing by comparing him to the Dixie Limited, her projection of his fictional power by means of a factual Southern express train proved both effective for her purposes and appropriate to his career and canon. Complicated junctions of actual and apocryphal railroads in both his life and work suggest a closer consideration of this topic within the contexts of Southern culture, Southern literature, and the Southern Renaissance. Finally, Yoknapatawpha's tracks and trains become complex cultural metaphors providing passages through territory we might call "darkest Faulkner"—the author's ambivalence, not just in regard to technology, but to class, gender, and race—particularly as revealed in the saga of the autobiographical Sartoris, Benbow, and Strother families.

The personal basis of Faulkner's railroad imagery begins even before his birth in 1897. During Reconstruction, the family patriarch, Colonel W.C. Falkner, turned his energies to the extension of a north/south rail link from his power base in Ripley, Mississippi. The variance in the spelling of the family patronymic was caused by the Colonel's dropping of the "u" and the author's restoration of it, both for reasons of self-assertion and separation from the past. Biographical and psychological critics have underlined the pervasive importance of this monumental forbear to Faulkner's life and work. An author of some repute in his region, Colonel Falkner began his own literary transformation into a Southern archetype; in a 1952 interview Faulkner speculated, "I may have inherited the ink stain from him" (Blotner, *Faulkner* 109). Indeed, this metaphorical inheritance may have been a sort of Rorschach blot in which the younger writer might discern the cultural baggage of his patrimony—both the creative urges and dark sins of the fathers, with their inevitable heritage of guilt, confusion, and conflict.

Colonel Falkner's most successful literary work remains his romance, *The White Rose of Memphis* (1881), which climaxes in a wild train ride from Grenada, Mississippi, to the title city. Written in the same period during which he sought political and financial backing for the extension of his Ripley railroad south to the Gulf and north to the Great Lakes, both Colonel Falkner's actual bestseller and his projected rail syndicate replicate the polar tensions between romanticized visions of the New South and its harsh historical realities. His great-grandson would discern these tensions personified in an ancestor credited with the creation of cavalry troops, railroad companies, and romantic heroines, but stained by rumors of smuggled contraband, legislative chicanery, repeated "miscegenation," and worse. The darkest reading of Colonel Falkner is found in Joel Williamson's study of his great-grandson's relation to Southern history, though Williamson still remains unable to demonstrate how much Faulkner actually knew about his great-grandfather's failings. My study assumes only the tensions evident in Faulkner's factual and fictional families, white and black.

Specifically in terms of railroad symbolism, my research for the present study confirms wide-spread brutality in the use of convict labor that belies a romanticized view of empire-building in the New South. For example, the family legend portrayed the Old Colonel talking northern Mississippi folks into a railroad much like the Music Man selling a marching band to River City (Williamson 50). In reality, the state of Mississippi's convicts of the 1880s were leased at $50 a year and board for labor "outside the walls." Well over a hundred prisoners a year, about 75 percent of them blacks, became the charges of the Gulf and Ship Island Railroad Company, one of the several incarnations of Colonel Falkner's railway projects (Lemley 287, 289). During those years the death rate of the leased convicts rose to better than 15 percent, compared to less than 1 percent "inside the walls" of the less than progressive prisons in the state of Mississippi (Jones 117, 128). Given the obvious incentives for mistreatment, including the agreement to return all prisoners "dead or alive," it seems difficult to credit the Colonel's response to legislative criticism that his convicts were treated as well as any laborers in the state of Mississippi (Williamson 51). Ironically, Colonel Falkner was shot to death in 1889 by a disaffected former partner in his railroad ventures and buried beneath his larger-than-life statue of Italian marble, which still faces his tracks and marks the limitations of his personal ambitions.

The monumental aspects of the Southern Renaissance have been questioned by its critics, from Richard King in the 1980s to Michael Kreyling and Richard Gray recently. In her study *Dirt and Desire: Reconstructing Southern Women's Writing,* Patricia Yaeger continues this interrogation, asking if the work done by women, blacks, and poor whites has not produced its own monuments in the plantations and the cities, or the river levees and railroads, using both folklore and the writing informed by it for examples (47–48, 113–14). Of course, her point is well taken, though we must recognize that it is not one ignored by the canonical writers of the Southern Renaissance: the statues of Colonel Sartoris and other Confederate soldiers in Faulkner's Jefferson, the stone figures on the Square in Wolfe's recreated Asheville, and the Civil War monuments in Warren's reminiscences and fiction all suggest a similar inquiry.

It should also be noted that railroads become conflicted images and symbols in black writing as well as white. Although the transforming train ride of Zora Neale Hurston's protagonist in *Jonah's Gourd Vine* may represent the positive elements of the Great Migration, neither the construction nor the utilization of the south/north rail lines lacked negative aspects. The black convicts who died in Colonel Falkner's dream of a Gulf to Great Lakes railroad, or those killed by a mountain railway disaster in John Ehle's fact-based 1964 novel, *The Road,* bear mute testimony to the sweat and blood shed by the poor blacks and whites who constructed literal and figurative monuments to similar patriarchal visions. Even those who migrated northward, both black and white, paid a high price on both ends of their epic journey.

The Ripley line represented a considerable family fortune, however, and it formed the basis of the Fa(u)lkner patrimony even after his son (known then by courtesy title as the Young Colonel) sold the property to a new Gulf/Chicago syndicate in 1903 (Lemley 289). The Young Colonel's son, Murray C. Falkner, William Faulkner's father, evidently wanted nothing more than to run the family railroad, and he worked his way up through the railroad ranks, serving as fireman, engineer, conductor, and finally station agent at New Albany, Mississippi, where William Faulkner was born. The loss of the family's railroad six years later proved a disappointment Murray never overcame, and his frustration at later career developments in Oxford, most notably as the business manager at Ole Miss, contributed to his estrangement from his son.

Young Billy Faulkner's fascination with trains was only a little stronger than that of most youngsters growing up in the first decade of the twentieth century. The railroad depot was the real heart of a town like Oxford in those days, when John Faulkner tells us "about half the town would meet the train to see who was coming in or leaving" (*My Brother Bill* 60). Billy made friends with the son of an Illinois Central engineer, who let the boys ride in the cab, sound the bell, and handle the throttle (Blotner, *Faulkner* 34). Like all his pals, young Faulkner could identify the engineer of an approaching train by the tones of its steam whistle, as "highballers on the old I. C." like Casey Jones had custom-made equipment mounted on their regular locomotives (Hansen 35). Even as he grew older and became more interested in automobiles and airplanes, Faulkner retained his romantic sense of railroads; for example, Ben Wasson recalled dinners with the budding author at the trackside Shack Café in Oxford during their college years, speculating on the destinations of passengers on the Pullmans gliding past (Wells 865).

2

Yoknapatawpha's railroads were created by Faulkner's imaginative merger of the Ripley railroad and the line that had been extended through Oxford in the antebellum years. In geographical terms, the author's fictive map of Yoknapatawpha County is stitched down the middle by the crosshatching of John Sartoris's railroad, much as the real map of Faulkner's native Lafayette County, Mississippi, was split by the actual Illinois Central Railroad (Duvert 14). In terms of chronology, Faulkner relocated the construction of the Sartoris railroad between that of its two actual models—the Oxford line in the 1850s and the Ripley railroad in the 1880s—placing his fictional construction project during Reconstruction in the 1870s, an important change in historical terms that conflates Reconstruction and the New South. Colonel Sartoris's dream of a Gulf to Great Lakes rail route represents no less than a romanticized reunification of South and North by means of the burgeoning technology.

The family saga that Faulkner began in 1927 under the poetic title *Flags in the Dust* presents similar, fitfully idealized images of Faulkners and Sartorises past and present, which were then revised for the slimmer family romance published in 1929 as *Sartoris*. The complicated publication history of Faulkner's first Yoknapatawpha novel created several textual problems; however, the two published versions will be viewed here as two parts of the same family story, following Douglas Day's introduction to the "reconstructed" *Flags in the Dust*. The Sartoris heritage is symbolized when old Bayard opens their ancient war chest to record his grandson John's death in aerial combat over the western front; the enclosed relics all prove aristocratic, dangerous, and/or masculine: "a rapier and a saber, dueling pistols and a 'der'nger,' a machete, and a long-necked oil can such as locomotive drivers use. It was of silver, and engraved upon it, surrounded by a carved ornate wreath, was the picture of a locomotive with a huge bell-shaped funnel. Beneath it, the name, 'Virginia' and the date, 'August 1873'" (*Sartoris* 91). Worth noting are the locomotive's name, suggestive of both the family's cavalier heritage and its romanticized traditions, as well as Colonel John's sister. Also, the engine's bell-like stack balances the

phallic thrust of the engine's boiler, as do the "long-necked" com-
memorative oil can and the several varieties of masculine and
destructive weaponry.

The imagery in this multigenerational treasure trove reifies
the Sartoris spirit in seemingly liberating but ultimately determining and destructive machines. While the opening of *Flags in
the Dust* hearkens back to the older avatar of the romanticized
dream, a wood-burning locomotive named for a woman, the conclusion of *Sartoris* looks forward to the faster and more fascinating automobile and airplane—experiments and indulgences
supported by the legacy of the railroad in both Faulkner's fiction
and in his biography. The spirit of old Colonel Sartoris still determines the family's history down to the lost airmen of the present
generation, just as his monumental statue still dominates the
landscape of the fertile valley from its pedestal above his railroad and the family cemetery—the final, symbolic setting of this
family saga that concludes with the burial ceremony for the autobiographical protagonist, the doomed young Bayard Sartoris.

This young aviator returns to his *patria* from the Great War
by train, significantly descending from it on the side away from
the platform, so as to escape the notice of the station loungers. As
Old Simon, their retainer, reports to the Sartoris household:
"Wouldn't even get off at the dee-po . . . de dee-po his own folks
built. Jumpin' ofen de bline side like a hobo" (*Flags* 10).

Young Bayard's other notable train ride in Yoknapatawpha
takes place on Christmas night while returning from the
MacCallums' isolated farm, where he retreated in a guilt-ridden
response to Old Bayard's fatal injury as a passenger in his road-
ster. The grandson's blind attempt to evade his own and his
family's past among poor white and black families in the scrubby
hills of Yoknapatawpha ends as the Sartoris railroad bears him
back to the family's own "silent box-like flag station" (*Sartoris*
154). The disheveled, drunken young Bayard reveals more than
a passing resemblance to his creator at this period in his development (Blotner, *Faulkner* 482, 556). His final flight from and
return to Jefferson are by train as well, as young Bayard deserts
his new bride and their unborn child to meet his suicidal fate in
Chicago and then find his final repose beneath the stone gaze of
John Sartoris's monumental statue.

By contrast, Horace Benbow, young Bayard's friend and foil, leaves Jefferson with his new bride, the divorcée Belle Mitchell, and his stepdaughter, Little Belle, to face a more mundane fate in the raw lumber town of Kinston, somewhere in the Delta. In material largely excised from *Flags in the Dust* in Ben Wasson's editing of *Sartoris,* Horace also returned from the Great War by train, bearing the artistic implements to create a delicate glass vase representing his aesthetic, fragile, and androgynous relationship with his sister Narcissa. After she impulsively marries young Bayard, he turns to the domineering Belle. Horace's family life is now ordered by the rhythm of trains arriving and departing at Kinston's "new, ugly yellow station" (*Flags* 401). The railroad provides his connection with the larger world, both his ambivalent flight from the repressed past represented by Narcissa in Jefferson and his fitful attempts to escape his repressive present represented by both Belles in Kinston. For example, each Tuesday afternoon he meets the northbound train to procure a case of Gulf shrimp for the delectation of his voracious wife, a demeaning errand that comes to stand for his reduced masculine role in his own mind.

Significantly, a night train's Jim Crow car returns the black draftee, Caspey Strother, from the war. The somewhat feckless scion of the Sartorises' servant and shadow family, Caspey's major role is as the dark, rejected brother to young Bayard. His re-education through a passage abroad suggests racial tensions that Faulkner will revisit more sympathetically in later fictions, but Caspey does not progress much beyond a stereotype whose wounds are earned in a "razor-hedged crap game" and whose proudest wartime honor was "getting his white" in France (*Sartoris* 62, 67). When his nominal father, Old Simon, cannot convince him of his "place," his white father figure, Old Bayard, clubs him into it with a stick of stove wood. Even the polite Miss Jenny invokes the historical risen "red neck," Senator Vardaman, who knew better than those in Washington "who thought of putting niggers into the same uniform with white men" (*Sartoris* 68). The cultural inevitability of these racial conflicts is connected closely with the South/North rail line, which brings black men like Caspey back and forth between smaller and larger, fated and free worlds. Finally, these rails come to symbolize a migration route as historically and psychologically significant in the New South as the Underground Railroad was in the old.

These three early incarnations—young Bayard Sartoris, Horace Benbow, Caspey Strother—become prototypes of characterizations that will appear and reappear in many guises and under many names throughout the Faulkner canon. In fact, they also may be considered as representative of three cultural "main lines" of class, gender, and race that can be followed throughout the saga of Yoknapatawpha, both geographically and historically considered. For example, the young Bayard Sartoris represents the lost protagonists like Quentin Compson, born beyond their day and condemned by the constrictions of class to their inevitable doom. We need only consider Bayard's patronymic: "there is death in the sound of it, and a glamorous fatality, like silver pennons downrushing at sunset, or a dying fall of horns along the road to Roncevaux" (*Sartoris* 40). Such knightly pretensions were common in the Old South: for example, Old Colonel Falkner was known during his days in the Confederate cavalry as "the Knight of the Black Plume" (Blotner, *Faulkner* 23). Such romanticized pretenses still existed into the modern South, though preserved in new guises such as Faulkner's own family romance.

3

Faulkner later reprised the matter of the Sartorises in his episodic novel, *The Unvanquished* (1938), which began as a series of lively stories intended for sale to popular magazines. The volume was formed into a larger narrative in Faulkner's first use of the short-fiction cycle, a genre employed again in *Go Down, Moses,* as we will see in chapter 4. As its very title suggests, *The Unvanquished* is constructed around cultural struggles based on binary cultural oppositions; if the Sartorises are to remain unvanquished, then others must be vanquished. During the war it is the enemy, the Yankees, in chapters titled "Ambuscade," "Retreat," and "Raid"; during Reconstruction, it becomes the new enemies—bushwhackers, carpetbaggers, and copperheads—in chapters of more ambiguous titles such as "Riposte in Tertio," "Vendee," and "Skirmish at Sartoris." Only in the seventh and final chapter, "An Odor of Verbena," does Bayard learn that the enemy is found much closer to home, indeed within his own family.

However, the overall narrative demonstrates that war and its aftermath are not significantly different, as both become unceasing struggles for control over the structures of cultural power, in both figurative and literal senses. An obvious example is the white columns and porticoes of the mansion, an almost universal symbolic structure in narratives as different as two epic novels published in 1936, Faulkner's *Absalom, Absalom!* and Margaret Mitchell's *Gone with the Wind.* After the Sartoris mansion is destroyed by the enemy during the war, the Colonel rebuilds it to mark the peace, "on the same blackened spot, over the same cellar, where the other had burned, only larger, much larger" (*Unvanquished* 220). Of course, the other important constructions are the postbellum railroads.

In the tales of the Civil War and Reconstruction that comprise *The Unvanquished,* Faulkner directly links such chivalric imagery with a daring locomotive chase based on the historical Andrews Raid (Stover, *American Railroads* 58): "It was like a meeting between two iron knights of the old time, not for material gain but for principle—honor denied with honor, courage denied with courage—the deed done not for the end but for the sake of the doing, put to the ultimate test and proving nothing" (*Unvanquished* 98). Faulkner's version of the Andrews Raid proves even less factual than versions by Buster Keaton, *The General* (1927), and by Walt Disney, *The Great Locomotive Chase* (1956), which at least keep the players and the sides straight. Faulkner makes the raid a doomed, chivalric Confederate initiative, ignoring both the ludicrous and the dreadful aspects of the actual chase; he was in the midst of his Hollywood screenwriting career when he penned the stories, perhaps with an eye toward screen rights, which accounts for the cinematic aspects of the writer's efforts.

As developed in chapter 1, the railroad here forms an interesting nexus between the idealization that justified the Civil War and the realpolitik that decided it. The limitations of rail transport in the antebellum South contributed as much as any single factor to the failure of secession, while postbellum construction by men like Nathan Bedford Forrest and William Clark Falkner, often with the backing of Yankee capital and technology, helped secure the successful resistance to Reconstruction in the South. The episodic narrative of *The Unvanquished* crosses some of Faulkner's most conflicted, evasive, and ambivalent considerations of class, gender, and race, combined with some of his most notable railroad images and symbols.

The most important of these cultural constructions proves to be the Sartoris railroad. Although much of the narrative reiterates material from the earlier Sartoris fictions, Faulkner adds a colorful recreation of the first train's triumphant arrival at Jefferson, in the words of the protagonist, the Old Bayard as a young man near the age of his grandson in the earlier books: "and Father in the cab blowing blast after blast on the whistle . . . and there were speeches at the station, with more flowers and a Confederate flag and girls in white dresses and red sashes and a band, and Father stood on the pilot of the engine and made a direct and absolutely needless allusion to Mr. Redmond" (*Unvanquished* 226). Redmond is the disabused former partner, vanquished in the economic struggle and here symbolically scorned from the Colonel's dominant position astride the iron horse that has replaced his war-time black stallion. However, the imagery of this heroic tableau, a sort of New South version of antebellum chivalry, bears on other cultural constructions as well. The Rebel flag recalls the "Old Cause," specifically the "irrecoverable gambit" (98) of the great locomotive chase: "the flaring and streaming smoke stack, the tossing bell, the starred Saint Andrews cross nailed to the cab roof, the wheels and the flashing driving rods on which the brass fittings glinted like the golden spurs themselves" (98). This cinematic treatment reinforces the aristocratic imagery of caparisoned chargers, fluttering pennons, and silvery trumpets, though here the overtones are more like D.W. Griffith's *The Birth of a Nation* (1915) than of later filmic incarnations by Buster Keaton and Walt Disney.

Gender constructions are also suggested by the flowers, white dresses, and red sashes of the maidens who greet the inaugural train. Interestingly enough, it is the androgynous Drusilla Hawk, later John Sartoris's young bride, who narrates the tale of the great locomotive chase—invoking her characteristic, inevitable sexual imagery—as she describes how the conspirators "would slip into the roundhouse in the dark to caress the wheels and pistons and the iron flanks to whisper to it in the darkness like lover to mistress or rider to horse" (*Unvanquished* 97). Drusilla also compares John Sartoris's dream to another fateful piece of machinery, "a loaded pistol with a hair trigger" (223), an intriguing image given her phallic association of the family's dueling pistols with "the physical shape of love" (227) as she presents them to Bayard in order to avenge his father's inevitable yet "honorable" death at the hands of his former partner.

Bayard's black companion, Ringo, completes the trilogy of class, gender, and race—both in terms of characterization and imagery. Ringo is inspired by the very idea of a railroad even before he has ever seen one; in particular, he is jealous of Bayard, who had viewed a train on an earlier trip to Hawkhurst, the seat of Drusilla's family in Alabama. Ringo makes the association of the ruined Rebel railroad they find near Hawkhurst with the implacable movement of the freed slaves in the wake of the Yankee raiders who destroyed it. "It was as if Ringo felt it too and that the railroad, the rushing locomotive which he hoped to see symbolized it—the motion, the impulse to move which had already seethed to a head among his people" (*Unvanquished* 81). These scenes of massed black humanity moving silently northward through the night remain the strongest in the book, perhaps because their motion suggests an immutable historical reality extending from the Underground Railroad to the modern black exodus in the Great Migration after the First World War.

These movements exist in sharp contrast to the frantic motions of the Sartoris dream imaged in the wild train rides considered earlier. Ringo's ironic contemplation of the rails near Hawkhurst—twisted into "Sherman's neckties" about the plantation's trees—evokes another "Disneyesque" diminution of the Sartoris vision, as he allows that the locomotive would "have to come in here and run up and down around those trees like a squirrel" (*Unvanquished* 88). By reducing this white patriarchal institution to a diminutive, toy-like scale, Ringo is engaged in the same sort of deconstruction that will mark many African American folk and literary treatments of Southern railroads.

By comparison, the powerful images of racial exodus do indicate, much like the startling sexual imagery that characterizes

Drusilla's telling of the family legends, that the essential constructions of culture are considered here in terms of class, gender, and race—much as in the earlier versions of the family saga, *Sartoris* and *Flags in the Dust*. Drusilla's phallic locomotive exists in a chivalric dream of the past, as does Ringo's vision of a liberating black exodus; the present is the reconstructed Sartoris railroad celebrating its inevitable progress into Jefferson, a small-scale version of the nation's self-congratulation at the joining of the east/west transcontinental railroad a few years earlier in 1869 (Stover, *American Railroads* 69).

In this single image, the local celebration in Jefferson conflates three historic railroad tableaux: the antebellum launching of the first trains, the war-time locomotive chases, and the postwar Golden Spike ceremonies. Taken by itself, the dramatic scene John Sartoris adumbrates might be equated with the Southern concept of "Redemption", the belief that events of the 1870s saved the South from Reconstruction, but Faulkner counts the real costs of cultural salvation (Nelson 179–82). The accounts would have to balance later, as Faulkner revised this family saga through the complicated and ambivalent stories of the intertwined McCaslin/Edmonds/Beauchamp family in *Go Down, Moses* (1942), as we will see in chapter 4.

Chapter Three

Thomas Wolfe's Southern Railroads

Look Homeward, Angel and Beyond

But so huge was the extent of my design . . . that I can liken
these chapters only to a row of lights which one sometimes
sees at night from the window of a speeding train, strung
out across the dark and lonely countryside.

Thomas Wolfe, *The Story of a Novel*

1

The connections between William Faulkner and Thomas Wolfe
are many, and they are complex. As this chapter and the next
will demonstrate, these relations include both personal and professional aspects in the lives and works of these two prolific writers, perhaps the two most important figures in the traditional
canon of the Southern Renaissance. One intriguing element common to both authors is their personal and literary interest in
Southern railroads, one remarked by critics of each writer but
not developed as yet within the fuller cultural context of Southern studies. This chapter will compare and contrast the real and
fictive trains of William Faulkner and Thomas Wolfe, moving from
Look Homeward, Angel to Wolfe's later fiction, and finally to the
larger contexts of Southern culture, Southern literature, and the
Southern Renaissance.

As a powerful historical force in the development of the modern South, the region's railroads were freighted with a complicated cultural content that was naturally inscribed in Southern
literature. As we have seen in chapter 1, the steam locomotive

represented the technologies that were transforming Dixie from an agrarian culture to an industrial society at the opening of the twentieth century. In general, the railroad as literary image and symbol represented the Southern cultural ambivalence in the face of these burgeoning technological intrusions—the inherent promises of freedom from the inertia of the fallen material world versus the threats of alienation from the traditional natural order. In other words, the railroad, like many new technologies of the twentieth century, represented both freedom and determinism for Southern culture. Once the train was boarded in the era of the New South, there was no getting off or going back until the regional journey to modernism, both cultural and literary, was finished.

William Faulkner, born in 1897, and Thomas Wolfe, born in 1900, grew up with the twentieth century and came of age, in literal and literary terms, during the 1920s and 1930s, the Golden Age of Southern railroading. Therefore, extending these patterns of cultural ambivalence in their lives and works will be our purpose in this chapter. William Faulkner's personal interest in trains came naturally enough to the heir of a regional railroad builder, so it also seems inevitable that his sagas of the Sartorises and the other biographical extended families in his later books are driven by steam locomotives. Thomas Wolfe's personal love of railroads is well known (Walser 3), and his professional use of railroad images and symbols is often remarked (Kimball 74); however, the pervasive motif of trains within the welter of his crowded, colorful, and frenetic personal life is not fully realized in his biography (Donald xv), while the ambivalence of his railroad imagery has been only suggested in the criticism of his voluminous fiction (Beja 34).

Indeed, consideration of Thomas Wolfe's real and recreated railroads raises difficult and complicated questions in regard to his place in the history and canon of Southern, American, and modern literatures. If William Faulkner's centrality to the traditional and canonical narrative of the Southern Renaissance calls the very construct into question for recent critics such as Michael Kreyling in his provocative study, *Inventing Southern Literature*, Thomas Wolfe's relation to Southern letters has always been problematic and somewhat marginalized. Although his home place in

Asheville, North Carolina, qualified him as a Southern writer for the New York literary establishment, his acceptance was not so ready in Dixie. The Fugitive/Agrarians, in particular, were always wary of Wolfe during his lifetime, raising questions concerning his mountain heritage, his rambling, rhetorical, and rather romantic earlier novels, and his relatively liberal politics in the later works. Not until the later reformulation of the Southern Renaissance by Louis Rubin Jr. and others after the Second World War was Wolfe admitted as a full-fledged member of the Southern pantheon (Kreyling 69).

In fact, Faulkner's literary sponsorship probably weighed as much in this reconsideration as Wolfe's genuine artistic merits. Although the two men only met once, they admired each other both personally and professionally; both seemingly appreciated and perhaps envied the early success of the other—Wolfe's popular acclaim and Faulkner's critical recognition. Wolfe admitted Faulkner's "imaginative and inventive power," granting him a significant place in Southern letters, and Faulkner put Wolfe at the head of his list for trying "to do the greatest of the impossible . . . to reduce all human experience to literature" (Donald 354). Even Faulkner's praise, however, suggests a reductive quality often attributed to Wolfe's work: the younger writer tried to do too much, and in the attempt seemed an interesting failure rather than an artistic success. Faulkner reneged on some of his praise and came to a more qualified position in regard to Wolfe after his early death, and it has been echoed in more recent criticism, along with the inevitable questions of canonical worthiness. William Faulkner's achievements have been questioned recently, while Thomas Wolfe's accomplishments are most often ignored or marginalized today.

One cause of this unfortunate development exists in the accessibility of Wolfe's work, access here understood in terms of texts rather than subject, style, or idea. Thomas Wolfe remains a wonderfully readable writer, more so in many ways than William Faulkner and many others in the traditional canon of the Southern Renaissance. He was a creator more than a craftsman, however, and the shaping of his massive manuscripts of poetic prose often fell to others for a number of extraliterary reasons. It remains beyond our purposes here to rehearse the complicated questions of Wolfe's publication history and textual problems. Suffice it to say that Wolfe's huge canon, literally millions of words in manuscript, is represented by four long books, called novels individually and collectively a tetralogy, as well as several volumes of shorter pieces variously named but rarely fashioned as such by the writer. Only one of the longer works, *Look Homeward, Angel,* can really be read as a novel; yet even this text was shaped from the longer and recently republished *O Lost!* (2000). The other three "novels" become more like fictional anatomies or anthologies assembled by Wolfe's erstwhile editors, Maxwell Perkins and Edward Aswell. Even his great first novel is a long, diffuse, and encyclopedic *Kunstlerroman*—not the sort of work much favored in the present literary climate, either popular or critical. Therefore, Thomas Wolfe is not so much reread as regarded by contemporary criticism, and regarded with suspicion derived from several generations of critics with personal, professional, and/or ideological scores to settle.

For example, Michael Kreyling's recent revisionist study proves typical in these considerations. Although William Faulkner's centrality is disputed in Kreyling's reconsideration of the Southern Renaissance, his reputation requires a full chapter and twenty more references to revise, while Thomas Wolfe is only mentioned four times. For the most part, these references to Wolfe are used to support Louis Rubin's alleged appropriation of Southern studies, with the help of henchmen like C. Hugh Holman. Rubin does receive some credit from Kreyling for trying to rescue Wolfe's literary repute—at least his quixotic gesture challenged the Fugitive/Agrarian hegemony—but finally Wolfe proves only another dead white male author of "hirsute" novels better left in the "literary boondocks" (40). Oddly, Wolfe resented just this attitude from his Fugitive/Agrarian critics, pointing out to them that he was the best educated, most deeply read, and most widely traveled among the major American writers of his day, not a romantic rube from the mountains. (Patricia Yaeger's consideration of Wolfe in *Dirt and Desire* proves even more perfunctory as she relegates him to an omnibus footnote: "It is my aim to displace the dominance of Faulkner, Percy, Warren, and Wolf [*sic*] with the voices of their brilliant female contemporaries" [279 n. 2].)

2

Despite Thomas Wolfe's self-confessed love of trains (*Letters* 624), the same powerful ambivalence concerning them obtains in his life and work as in Faulkner's. Indeed, railroad references increase in his later fictions, but this pattern can be discerned in and extended from his first and best, *Look Homeward, Angel.* This novel presents some of the most arresting images of his ambivalent fascination with and fear of technology in the guise of railroads. The first long train ride of the autobiographical Eugene Gant to St. Louis for the World's Fair of 1904 is imaged as a dream journey across mountains and rivers: "Eugene watched the sun wane and redden on the rocky river, and on the painted rocks of the Tennessee gorges: the enchanted river wound into the child's mind forever. Years later, it was to be remembered in dreams tenanted with an elfish and mysterious beauty. Stilled in great wonder, he went to sleep to the rhythmical pounding of the heavy wheels" (*Angel* 44). Later, at the fair itself, his older sister Daisy takes young Eugene for a ride on a frightening scenic railway, a journey filled with "insane horrors" for the little boy, like "a fabulous nightmare" (46). The most arresting image at the fair, however, is found among the exhibits of innovative technology. "Once in a huge building roaring with sound, he was rooted before a mighty locomotive, the greatest monster he had ever seen, whose wheels spun terrifically in grooves, whose blazing furnaces, raining hot red coals into the pit beneath, were fed incessantly by two grimed fire-painted stokers. The scene burned in his brain like some huge splendor out of Hell: he was appalled and fascinated by it" (46). Eugene's youthful epiphany recalls Henry Adams's vision before the huge dynamo at another technological fair only a few years earlier; though the boy's reaction is more emotional than intellectual, he experiences the same fascination and fear at this revelation of the technological fate born with the new century.

Eugene Gant's developing railroad images extend these conflicted feelings to the regional problems of gender, race, and class. Following paternal examples of long rail wanderings, Eugene yearns to escape from hill-pent Altamont, so that his train trips at first seem wonderful flights from reality. Yet they all end in human frustration, as with the death of his brother Grover, which brings the Gants home from the St. Louis fair with his little body in the baggage car (*Angel* 49). At the end of the novel's part 1, Eugene's movement from childhood to adolescence is marked by train trips across the Southern states—to resorts in Tampa, Hot Springs, New Orleans, Savannah—in the company of his restless mother, voyages in which he intuits the romantic, sexual subtexts of his travel fantasies, of "the South which burned like dark Helen in Eugene's blood . . . the core and desire of dark romanticism" (127).

Part 2 of *Look Homeward, Angel* concludes with Eugene's first trip without his mother, to Charleston, South Carolina, down Saluda grade, the steepest on the Southern railroad: "His mind was bound in the sad lulling magic of the car wheels" (*Angel* 297), as earlier, then across South Carolina by night toward his first, frustrated romantic stirring with the little waitress, Louise. In realistic contrast, train 36 with engineer Tom Cline at the throttle, "with short explosive thunders began to climb Saluda. She bucked helplessly like a goat, her wheels spun furiously on the rails. She slipped, spun, held, ploughed slowly up, like a straining mule, into the dark" (139). In part 3, Eugene follows his lost love, the newly married Laura, in this instance to Norfolk and a job in the wartime shipyards. Upon his arrival by train, Eugene thinks the locomotive as "beautiful as any ship" (426), though this voyage ends in the romantic frustration of dull shipyard days and drunken nights.

Like William Faulkner, Thomas Wolfe moves his railroad images closer to cultural formulations. Notable examples in Faulkner include the conflicted considerations of class, gender, and race personified by young Bayard Sartoris, feckless Horace Benbow, and disaffected Caspey Strother. In *Look Homeward, Angel,* Eugene Gant's insights are glimpsed from the window of a speeding train. "He heard the ghostly ticking of his life . . . plucking out of the ghostly shadows a million gleams of light—a little station by the rails at dawn, the road cleft through the pineland seen at twilight, a smoky cabin-light below the trestles, a boy who ran bounding among the calves, a wisp-haired slattern, with snuff-sticked mouth, framed in a door, floury negroes unloading sacks from freight-cars on a shed . . ." (*Angel* 159). Both the sounds and sights aboard the speeding trains become insights into the tense balance of change and fixity for Eugene and his creator: "the terrible moment of immobility stamped with eternity in which passing life at great speed, both the observer and the observed seem frozen in time" (159). For a moment, nothing moves—land, train, slattern, Eugene—then "fixed in no-time, the slattern vanished, fixed, without a moment of transition" (159).

The development of railroads, along with other technologies of the nineteenth century, undoubtedly influenced twentieth-century modernism, as we noted in chapter 1. The power and speed of railroads not only affected modernist themes such as the sense of disconnection and alienation, but they also affected modernist style in its use of fragmentation, juxtaposition, and montage—as, for example, in the passages quoted above. In turn, the Southern Renaissance traditionally has been defined by the confluence of Southern matter with the modernist manner. So Wolfe's scenes here are somewhat like photographs, or even more like "motion-pictures," which can freeze or speed the action in his Southern scenes and narratives (*Angel* 159). In both photography and film, modern technology provides new ways to pose ancient questions, as well as innovative methods to frame new insights or answers.

Other American writers—William Faulkner and F. Scott Fitzgerald in fiction, Hart Crane and Allen Tate in poetry, Eugene O'Neill and Elmer Rice in drama—as well as American artists in other media: Edward Hopper and Charles Burchfield in painting, Alfred Stieglitz and Walker Evans in photography, D.W. Griffith and John Ford in film—all struggled with the same materials and methodologies. Interestingly enough, all of these artists employ trains as major symbols of the cultural changes that were the very stuff of their works, and, even more importantly, they all discovered a similar cultural ambivalence. William Faulkner's *Sartoris* and Thomas Wolfe's *Look Homeward, Angel* are but two examples, though very representative ones, of the ambivalent readings of the railroad, of technology, and of modern culture in terms of gender, race, and class provided by the best American and Southern literature and art in the exhilarating decade of the "roaring Twenties."

3

By way of contrast, the Depression decade of the 1930s witnessed significant changes in American and Southern culture, art, and literature, which in turn impacted the works of all these writers. In a climate of criticism somewhat parallel to the present, the social commitment of Faulkner, Wolfe, and others in the traditional canon of the Southern Renaissance came under critical scrutiny and suspicion. As the Depression worsened, Faulkner was regarded as the high modernist historian of Southern degeneracy and grotesquerie, while Wolfe was considered the post-Romantic celebrant of solipsism and sensuality. In all of this rereading, emphasis had shifted from self to society in literary matter and from modernist mannerism to social realism in literary form. These critical reactions by their contemporaries can be justified by some aspects of these authors' early efforts, much like the critical interrogation of their works by recent revisionists in terms of the new correctness. These critical exercises in both the past and the present, however, seek to fit the works of individualistic, imaginative, and iconoclastic writers like Faulkner, Wolfe, and many others in the traditional canon of the Southern Renaissance into procrustean patterns of matter and form, image and symbol, theme and meaning.

First of all, we must recognize that all of these writers were sensitive to the developments around them and that their later works evolved in response to a changing world. For this reason, William Faulkner's later fictions, especially *Go Down, Moses,* will be the subject of chapter 4, while Robert Penn Warren's later poetry will focus chapter 7. Wolfe, still young, sensitive, and vital during the 1930s, made the most conscious effort to reconsider his matter and form from these new perspectives. These changes are nowhere more evident than in his use of railroad images and symbols. Even as railroad imagery becomes ever more pervasive in his writing, Wolfe's emphasis shifts from the Southern prototypes of his past to the Northern, Western, and European trains of his present. Of course, these new subject matters are to some extent determined by his own biography as he ranges outside his Southern homeland, but their literary treatment develops as well, becoming more social, more realistic, and more insightful in terms of their relation to his own past.

Thomas Wolfe's second "novel," *Of Time and the River,* continues the development of the autobiographical Eugene Gant. He travels north, after graduating from his Southern state university, to study at Harvard, to teach and write in New York City, and to sail for Europe. His new journey starts with a northward train ride from Altamont to Boston lasting more than eighty pages; indeed, at one point Wolfe planned an entire novel around such a journey under the working title *K-19,* the number of the Southern Railroad's Pullman car on the overnight express run from Asheville to New York. Eugene, of course, is not much changed at this starting point in the narrative. He is still given to rhapsodic recreations of the railroad journey: "It seemed to him these two terrific negatives of speed and stillness, the hurtling and projectile movement of the train and the calm silence of the everlasting earth, were poles of a single unity—a unity coherent with his own destiny, whose source was somehow in himself" (*Time* 35). Also familiar are his sardonic takes on fellow passengers from Altamont, his drunken antics with former college friends, and his romantic/sexual fantasies about the night train: "It is the place where the women with fine legs and silken underwear lie in the pullman berth below you" (155).

As this long, diffuse, and discursive narrative unfolds, train journeys provide more narrative pace and order than the title's symbol of the river, so that Wolfe might have more honestly titled it *Of Time and the Railroad.* Indeed, for a careful reader, a notable image of a huge urban railway terminus makes just such a suggestion: "unutterable in unceasing movement and in changeless change as the great river is, and time itself" (*Time* 245). Eugene must come home by train after his Harvard years, traveling South once again for the death and funeral of his father, a more sobering and enlightening journey, though still ordered by the romanticized visions similar to those encountered earlier in his first novel. "Father, in the night time, in the dark, I have heard the thunder of the fast express" (333). Returning to New York with a race between speeding trains across the New Jersey meadows, Wolfe seems to connect the craft of the locomotive driver with his own (407). Eugene later boards the Limiteds of the New

York Central in the Hudson Valley to escape the city and visit wealthy, effete, and patronizing friends at their country homes, replete with miniature garden railways. Finally, Wolfe's surrogate rides the railroads of England and France, which provide a different vision of the world than the trains of his youth.

Stung by criticism from Robert Penn Warren and others, which called his first two novels merely romanticized autobiography, Wolfe resolved to distance himself from his own life by creating a different protagonist, George Webber. The narrative development of his central character retold the story of the artist trying to find himself in the South, the North, and Europe. Although he had some editorial control over his first two books, Wolfe's death in 1938 left his publishers with a huge manuscript from which editor Edward Aswell unsuccessfully tried to conjure the "Great American Novel." *The Web and the Rock* (1939*)* and *You Can't Go Home Again* (1940) are crowded with tracks and trains that convey the same sense of modern technological ambivalence, but they are more carefully treated in terms of the contradictions of gender, race, and class.

Examples from both books illustrate the evolution of Wolfe's vision between the Eugene Gant and George Webber sequences. Although the protagonist's rail journeys in *The Web and the Rock* roughly parallel Eugene Gant's in the first fictional sequence, George Webber's are less restricted in range, less romanticized in matter, and, at the same time, less modernist in manner. For example, presenting his protagonist's aesthetic reactions to highbrow, abstractionist, and modernist art in *The Web and the Rock,* Wolfe has Webber know at some deep level of his consciousness that, by contrast, "freight cars were beautiful; that a spur of rusty boxcars on a siding, curving off somewhere into a flat of barren pine and clay, was as beautiful as anything could be, as anything has ever been" (*Web* 247).

At the opening of *You Can't Go Home Again,* George makes a sad journey south from Manhattan for the funeral of Aunt Maw, the surrogate mother who raised him, speculating on time and change in Pennsylvania Station, entertaining romantic fantasies, and encountering the same businessmen and boosters Eugene had observed. Wolfe's earlier observations had remained merely satirical, but here attention focuses on the Faulknerian figure of

Judge Rumford Bland, the scion of an old family who makes his money in usurious lending to the black population of Libya Hill. His narrator's realization, not just of the failed patriarchy but of the plight of the poor whites and blacks in the early days of the Depression, takes him back to reconsider race and class relations, for example in the powerful biography of black rebel Dick Prosser in "The Child by Tiger," from *The Web and the Rock.*

In *You Can't Go Home Again,* the long sequence entitled "The Party at Jack's" combines imagery of subterranean rail lines and the vertical movement of elevators in a modernist manner employed by other writers of the Southern Renaissance, including Allen Tate, William Faulkner, and Ralph Ellison. The kitchen fire that disturbs the avant-garde spectacle of Esther Jack's artistic soiree, significantly enough a performance piece reenacting a tiny circus by the avant-gardist Piggy Logan, creating a virtual carnival of surreal action within the penthouse apartment and in the building's court bellow. The fire department's overreaction stops both subways and elevators, inconveniencing the rich dilettantes but killing two hapless workers. Wolfe's ironically unsympathetic portrait of his Jewish host and hostess makes contemporary critics understandably nervous, but the book ends with the recognition of Hitler's burgeoning anti-Semitism, the first in serious American literature.

Another train journey focuses George's revelation in the sequence "I Have a Thing to Tell You." Leaving Germany after the 1936 Olympics, George contemplates a *Reichsbahn* locomotive at the Belgian border: "Every line of this intricate and marvelous apparatus bore evidence of the organizing skill and engineering genius that had created it" (49). Later, Wolfe's protagonist watches with growing horror as a Jewish refugee is removed with comparable skill and efficiency from their shared compartment for trying to smuggle out money from the Reich. As the train steams away and he watches the figure of the little man on the station platform at the Belgian border recede into obscurity, George remembers all he has known of Southern prejudice, segregation, and lynching, even in his beloved home state of "Old Catawba," which Eugene earlier judged superior to the racist mores of the Deep South.

Thomas Wolfe was still evolving as a person and as an artist at the moment of his untimely death shortly before his thirty-eighth birthday. As always, his development was evidenced in the cultural use of railroads in his writing; George Webber puts it succinctly: "One's own sense of manhood and of mastery is heightened by being on a train" (*Can't Go Home* 49). Wolfe's quest for objectivity involved both self and other, as he struggled to come to terms with the world changing around him. William Faulkner was involved in similar contests in both life and literature; he lived on to become an ever more complex man and writer, the complicated central figure in both the construction of Southern Renaissance and its deconstruction by revisionist critics, as we will see in chapter 4.

Chapter Four

William Faulkner's Cultural Geography

Railroads in *Go Down, Moses*

There were railroads in the wilderness now . . .

William Faulkner, *Big Woods*

1

As we discovered in chapter 2, William Faulkner's railroad images and symbols can be traced from his own family history to the Sartoris family saga, his very first evocations of Yoknapatawpha. Other interesting, important railroads, both factual and fictional, abound, both within and without the geography of his mythic postage stamp of native soil. We can make further distinctions among the more traditional earlier materials, the "high modernist" period between the two Compson novels, and the later work that balances these modes with new considerations of gender, race, and class parallel to those discovered in the later fictions of Thomas Wolfe. Given this chronological and geographical arrangement, *Go Down, Moses* (1942) proves the capstone of Faulkner's major phase, the keystone of the Yoknapatawpha narrative, and the cornerstone of an extended Southern Renaissance. As we might expect, no text in the Faulkner canon is more profoundly focused by the railroads in its landscape than this pivotal publication at the cultural transition between the Depression decade and the Second World War. Like the later works of Thomas Wolfe, the many trains discovered in *Go Down, Moses* demonstrate a maturing writer coming to terms with his own ambivalence, not just toward technology, landscape, and geography, but toward larger issues of gender, race, and class in Southern culture.

Go Down, Moses reconfigures Southern cultural ambivalence about gender, race, and class through the entangled interracial genealogy of the McCaslin/Edmonds/Beauchamp family. Of course, genealogy, like history, proves another cultural construct, one both determined by and mirrored in the shaping and stewardship of the land. Faulkner's contrapuntal narrative relates historical complexities to geographical ones and gender, racial, and class concerns to environmental ones (Wittenberg 49). Railroads shape Yoknapatawpha's landscape as much as any single historical factor, and these technological constructions have also determined much of the region's cultural geography. A dark record of environmental degradation and human exploitation is revealed by the network of real and recreated railroads Faulkner weaves into the complicated narrative patterns of *Go Down, Moses*.

As in the actual Mississippi of his youth and manhood, Faulkner's apocryphal rail lines grid the landscape in response to both the natural shape of the land and the shaping pressures of culture. As witness, we have his own map of Yoknapatawpha, stitched down the middle by the crosshatching of the Sartoris railroad (Duvert 14). Like his region's river systems, the rail lines' prevailing axis is south/north, stretching toward the Gulf or the Ohio, while east/west branches, often tracing tributary streams, gather and disperse freight and passengers to and from the trunk lines. Even as civilization penetrated the last of the "Big Woods" with branch-line logging railroads, African Americans began leaving the countryside of the South up the main lines to the cities of the North. The movement of the Underground Railroad of the nineteenth century extended into the Great Migration of the twentieth century, changing cultures at both ends of the epic journey, as recent scholarship on race and culture in Southern literature has demonstrated (Lester 123).

This geographical pattern is discernible in the spatial ordering of the title piece, "Go Down, Moses," which in its final position also provides a coda for the volume. This dual title, borrowed from one of the best-known black spirituals, suggests many layers of intertextual meaning—literary, historical, religious, and cultural.

Furthermore, the spiritual also creates spatial and geographical dichotomies that Faulkner elaborates in his counterpointed narratives. In this one, the baggage car of southbound "Number Four" bears down home to Jefferson the body of Butch Beauchamp, a black numbers runner executed after a deadly shootout with the Chicago police. Ironically, when the condemned black man was interviewed in his cell before his execution, he confessed only to "getting rich too fast" (370).

After briefly viewing the condemned man awaiting his fate, the story shifts southward to Yoknapatawpha where his grandmother, her white patrons—Miss Worsham and Lawyer Stevens—and several others in the community conspire to return his remains for burial on the old place from which young Butch had been banished for stealing from the commissary. In Aunt Molly's view, "Roth Edmonds sold my Benjamin. Sold him in Egypt. Pharaoh got him" (371). The reader is ready to accept her judgment after witnessing Roth deny his own biracial progeny in the preceding chapter, "Delta Autumn," much as L.Q.C. McCaslin did several generations earlier.

The concluding funeral procession therefore reverses and deconstructs the motif of northbound escape and success in Southern and African American history and literature, much like the historically and geographically parallel work of Richard Wright. It also caps the development of increasingly rebellious and therefore culturally dissonant black male characters central in "Was," "The Fire and the Hearth," and "Pantaloon in Black," the narrative triad that opens *Go Down, Moses* and foregrounds the African American heritage struggling to assert itself within a dominant white culture. It is interesting to note that critical attention, which traditionally focused on the three wilderness tales—"The Old People," "The Bear," and "Delta Autumn"—recently has shifted away from them to the racial narratives as the thematic heart of the volume.

This shift in emphasis is motivated by revisionist thinking in terms of race, but it began in earlier generic considerations. The publication history of *Go Down, Moses*—as a recasting of "twice-told tales"—engendered a scholarly dialogue concerning its narrative identity as either a collection or a novel. Earlier criticism, in its emphasis on the centrality of "The Bear," leaned toward the collection; later readings emphasizing the racial tales judge it a novel. Faulkner argued against using "and Other Stories" in the title, suggesting that we might view it in the medial genre of a short-fiction cycle in the mode of Sherwood Anderson's *Winesburg, Ohio* (1919), Ernest Hemingway's *In Our Time* (1925), or John Steinbeck's *The Long Valley* (1938) (Millichap 7).

John Carlos Rowe's interesting, insightful discussion of *Go Down, Moses* incorporated in his recent study *At Emerson's Tomb: The Politics of Classic American Literature* (222) makes a case for reading the overall narrative as a novel. Although the critic gives Faulkner credit for trying to include the African American presence, story, and voice, he sees the book as a failure in comparison with comparable works by black writers. However, his reading neglects Faulkner's larger purpose of trying to recreate the dialogic racial voices of the Delta, just as his analysis scants the hunting camp dialogues in the wilderness chapters and never mentions the multiracial oral traditions of Sam Fathers.

Finally, Rowe overplays his hand with the trump card of revisionist criticism; disagreement with his reading implies an undeveloped political consciousness. By privileging the racial chapters and relating them to texts by black writers with different agendas, "we discover how our own habits of professional reading imitate and thus redouble Faulkner's own tendency to repeat the will-to-power of the Southern white landed estate" (229). My reading tries to hear all the dialogic voices in *Go Down, Moses,* and I believe this is the position of many white and black readers in regard to the Yoknapatawpha fictions, including Ralph Ellison and Toni Morrison, both of whom create narrative and critical texts significantly intertextual with Faulkner's, as we will see later in this chapter and in chapter 7.

2

As an example of the internal intertextualities in *Go Down, Moses,* disaffected African American women depart on northbound trains at countered points in the two narrative strands. In "The Fire and the Hearth," McCaslin Edmonds drives his tenant Oscar's "yellow slut" to Jefferson and buys her train ticket northward, ostensibly to keep the peace on the plantation, as old Lucas

Beauchamp reminds him (119). Given Edmonds's own history of interracial love affairs, his motivation may be more personal. In "Delta Autumn," the last panel in the triptych of hunting stories that form the wilderness sequence of the novel, Edmonds coldly denies his light-skinned African American lover and their infant son, evidently conceived during their sojourn in Arizona almost a year earlier. Left with only his conscience money, she repudiates the Beauchamp inheritance. Her cousin will take her to the north-bound train at Leland (361), an actual junction in the Delta, after she accepts old Ike McCaslin's symbolic gift of a hunting horn, which ironically represents the now corrupted wilderness heritage. North/south railroads thus punctuate "Delta Autumn," the penultimate piece in the volume, prefiguring the ironic and elegiac mood of the concluding title narrative.

In a crucial passage, Faulkner italicizes the prose to indicate its location in the consciousness of Ike McCaslin, the central persona and a Faulkner surrogate in several senses—including Ike's ambivalent attitudes toward his patriarchal heritage, represented in his family's conflicted genealogy and by the Delta's depleted landscape. *"This land which man has deswamped and denuded and delivered in two generations so that white men can own plantations and commute every night to Memphis and black men can own plantations and ride in jim crow cars to Chicago to live in millionaires' mansions on Lakeshore Drive where white men rent farms and live like niggers and niggers crop on shares and live like animals"* (364). Among the many ironies evident here, it seems doubtful that as many black emigrants became rich at the cost of degrading the landscape and exploiting its people in their economic bondage to an extractive agriculture as did white planters; more realistic are the codified incivilities of segregated rail travel as the cost of doing business within the binary cultural constructs of the Delta. However, Faulkner's capsule history of the Delta has been confirmed by contemporary cultural historians; in particular, James C. Cobb's study, *The Most Southern Place on Earth: The Mississippi Delta and the Roots of Regional Identity,* devotes a chapter to Delta literature, including Faulkner's "Delta Autumn" and Eudora Welty's *Delta Wedding* (1946), which proves most effective at showing the Delta as a microcosm of the South, especially as a sort of staging ground

for the Great Migration pulling restless blacks from their traditional home places into proximity with the Illinois Central's main-
line to Chicago (184–208).

Another minority ethnic group historic to the Delta, "The
Old People" of the first wilderness tale's title, are recalled in "Delta
Autumn" through the other notable image of railroads following
the rivers' plains—the land across which there comes now no
scream of panther but instead the long hooting of locomotives:
"trains of incredible length . . . drawn by a single engine, since
there was no gradient anywhere and no elevation save those
raised by forgotten aboriginal hands" (341). This implied juxtaposition of earthwork constructions from these two cultures—
the sacred Indian mounds and the secular embankments of the
railroads—demonstrates not just their historical succession but
the economic determinism of the cultural competition between
them, a tension reinforced in the racial chapters with profane
uses of the mounds by both whites and blacks. The mile-long
freight trains are in a sense carrying off the belief systems of
native and minority cultures as well as the raw materials and
restless populations of the region. The chapter's autumnal title
suggests an elegy for this lost land and these lost peoples, moving from the freedom of the wilderness life to the environmental
death and cultural decay of the saw mill and sharecropping systems. James C. Cobb's cultural history of Delta also makes the
interesting point that the failure of the old systems of land ten-
ancy in the Depression created a colony of the welfare state, or a
sort of rural slum, a development that Faulkner decried from the
1940s on (329–33).

3

However, the east/west railroads, with their suggestions of another archetypal American journey, pervade all three of the hunting stories. Some African Americans trailed the displaced Native
Americans to the West from the post–Civil War South. For example, Fonsiba Beauchamp follows her husband, an unnamed
black preacher pioneering a westward promised land represented
by his father's freedman's pension of forty acres and a mule. By
the time young Ike McCaslin tracks them by train, stagecoach,

and horseback in a vain attempt to deliver old Carothers's legacy and thus expatiate his own guilt, they are raising a single hog on a squalid patch in the Arkansas Delta, a place symbolically named Midnight. Ike asks the preacher, "What corner of Canaan is this?" (279), a question that makes another allusion to biblical geography and might serve as an epigraph for Faulkner's volume.

Significantly enough, Toni Morrison's most recent novel, *Paradise* (1997), concerns the history of just such a utopian African American colony further west in Oklahoma founded by black migrants from the Deep South in the later nineteenth century. Although her narrative is factually based, one of Morrison's fictional black families is named Beauchamp, creating some intertextuality with Faulkner (the subject of her master's thesis) in terms of historical and geographical ironies inherent in the relations of race, gender, and class in the twentieth century. Another woman writer who uses the Beauchamp name, as well as the Delta setting, is Faulkner's fellow Mississippian, Eudora Welty. A number of other details—such as symbolically employed trains, confrontations in plantation commissaries, and biblical imagery—make Welty's *Delta Wedding* (1946) also seem intertextual with *Go Down, Moses*. Chapter 6 will develop Welty's views on these similar materials provided by the culture of the Delta.

Thematic irony is emphasized in the hunting stories of *Go Down, Moses* through frequent journeys on an east/west logging railroad that provides entry points into the last wilderness. This log-line snakes its way into the big woods from the junction at the lumber camp of Hokes, transporting out in small increments raw lumber that will later freight the long north/south trains. In the third section of "The Bear," Ike McCaslin and Boon Hogganbeck ride the logging train's caboose, "out of the woods under the paling east" (230), into Hokes to catch the mainline passenger connection northward on a whiskey run to Memphis. Although at first glance this anecdote of several pages seems only comic relief, it reinforces the tale's and the volume's contrast of wilderness and civilization while prolonging the suspense of the great bear hunt itself. Evidently, a good deal of this detail has its basis in Faulkner's own experience at similar Delta hunting camps in his youth, adulthood, and old age. Even the Memphis sojourn prefiguring the late comic epic *The Reivers* (1962) seems to have some autobiographical reference and relevance for the writer. Geographer Charles S. Aiken shows how Faulkner used three actual settings in the narrative and also suggests further bibliography on the cultural geography of the region (446–59).

The direction of Ike's train ride is reversed in the fifth section of "The Bear," after Major DeSpain "sold the timber rights to a Memphis lumber company" (316). Ike revisits the big woods to pay his respects to the tutelary spirits of the wilderness by bringing his votive offering to the grave of Sam Fathers, his multiracial mentor in the wilderness novitiate of the hunting camps. Reaching Hokes, he is bewildered by the erection of a new planing-mill and by "miles and miles of steel rails red with the bright rust of newness and of piled crossties sharp with creosote" (318). It is as if the westbound train "had brought with it into the doomed wilderness even before the actual axe the shadow and portent of the new mill not finished yet and the rails and ties which were not even laid" (321). Certainly, Ike's vision replicates the archetypal scene of modern machine invading traditional American garden.

On past trips the "little locomotive" with "its shrill peanut-parcher whistle" showed "the toylike illusion of crawling speed" (320). This cartoonlike quality was illustrated in the earlier anecdote of the young bear treed by the passing engine, in comic contrast to the breathless hunt for Old Ben. At least part of this contrast seems to rely on a tension of scale, like that which exists between actual and toy trains; Faulkner plays with the scale of trains in texts as varied as *As I Lay Dying* (1930), *The Unvanquished* (1938), and *The Reivers* (1962). In terms of another interesting intertextuality, Thomas Wolfe, Robert Penn Warren, Eudora Welty, and Dave Smith all make use of toy trains as symbolic markers contrastive to their full-scale prototypes in their fictional and poetic narratives.

During Ike's final trip, the engine moves with "deep slow clapping bites of power . . . like a small dingy harmless snake" (318), for the wilderness still looms "longer than any spur-line" (322). Leaving the woods, Ike confronts the avatar of all rattlesnakes, a totemic presence he ambivalently addresses in "the old tongue" as "Chief . . . Grandfather" (330). Among the many suggestions here are the paradoxical relationship between material and visionary power. On a material plane a locomotive may portend the despoiling of the big woods, but on a visionary level wilderness values exist beyond the immediate threat of the logging train, lumber mill, and the destruction that will follow in their wake.

Patricia Yaeger focuses on Ike McCaslin's last day in the field in her iconoclastic second chapter of *Dirt and Desire: Reconstructing Southern Women's Writing.* In particular, she asserts: "The train tracks that William Faulkner describes in *Go Down, Moses* furnish fuel for older readings of southern literature; they fan Agrarian flames" (35). Although her overall purpose, desegregating the white, male, middle-class symbolism of trains with Zora Neale Hurston's *Jonah's Gourd Vine,* proves laudable here, her reading of the logging line needs more contextual reading in terms of Faulkner's wilderness narratives, as demonstrated above and below. The citation of the protagonist's complex and powerful railroad imagery complements, not contradicts, Faulkner's, as Hurston's John Pearson discovers the train as "a glorified thing. . . . The greatest accumulation of power he had ever seen" (36). The south/north rail lines adumbrate this ambivalent power in white texts, such as African American chapters in *Go Down, Moses,* and in black ones, in those authored by females such as Welty and O'Connor, as well as by males like Wolfe or Faulkner.

An extended version of just this sort of power interchange takes place in the first three sections of "The Bear." Ike thrice images Old Ben, the granddaddy of all bears, in terms of a steam locomotive, once in each of the three opening sections. First, the archetypal bear runs through Ike's dreams, in an initiatory vision of "a corridor of wreckage and destruction beginning back before the boy was born, through which sped, not fast but rather with the ruthless and irresistible deliberation of a locomotive, the shaggy, tremendous shape" (193). After relinquishing the trappings of civilization for the archetypal hunt, Ike encounters Old Ben at last: "The bear rushed through rather than across the tangle of trunks and branches as a locomotive would, faster than he had ever believed it could have moved" (211). Finally, during the climactic chase, Ike imagines the great bear for the final time, "the thick locomotive-like shape that he had seen that day four years ago crossing the blow-down, crashing on ahead of the dogs faster than he had believed it could have moved" (238). It seems clear from these repetitive passages that Ike, like his creator, images both material and natural power in terms of a speeding locomotive. In these cross-cultural images, Ike McCaslin becomes both the last legatee of the old patriarch of the plantation, Carothers McCaslin, and the last initiate of the "old people" under the tutelage of his multiracial paternal surrogate, Sam Fathers, the last "Man" or Chief. He then returns the cultural power usurped by the inroads of civilization to the wilderness vision through the totemic symbol of the great bear, Old Ben, and the archetypal symbolism of the final hunt.

4

Of course, it becomes ironic that such "sacramental" readings of Faulkner's narrative, volume, and canon were first suggested by his earliest important critics like Fugitive/Agrarians and New Critics such as Allen Tate, Robert Penn Warren, and Cleanth Brooks, who drew analogies with American fictionists such as Herman Melville and Nathaniel Hawthorne as well as American thinkers like Henry Adams and William James. In particular, we should note intertextualities with two important works from these earlier American writers: Herman Melville's *Moby Dick* (1851) and Henry Adams's *Autobiography* (1907), both written in reaction to the technical transformation of American culture before and after the Civil War. Faulkner's old bear and new locomotive exist in a tension of nature and technology, much like Melville's great white whale and Ahab's dark whale ship, or Adams's medieval Virgin and modern Dynamo.

Faulkner, like his literary forebears, seems to posit a distinction between spiritual and material energy as they impact the creation of cultural power. The energies of nature may be determined, distorted, and denigrated in the artificial construction of gender, race, and class by the culture's power brokers. However, the restoration of natural power exists within the wilderness vision. The iron laws of segregation discovered in the narratives of racial confrontation disappear in the wilderness sequence of *Go Down, Moses,* where Ike learns from the oral traditions of the camp's white, black, and multiracial hunters. In the pivotal fourth section of "The Bear," where the fallen heritage of the plantation, rather than the Edenic vision of the wilderness, obtains, Ike experiences his most important epiphany reading the ledger books in the plantation commissary, texts which, like Faulkner's or Welty's fictions, reveal the degeneration of regional geography and history in the exploitation of land and people.

Ike then repudiates the heritage of his patriarchal ancestor, Old Carothers McCaslin, symbolized by the plantation, and—by way of the biographical extension to Old Colonel Falkner—the railroad. Daniel Singal connects the old bear and the Old Colonel (*William Faulkner* 283), but Louis J. Rubin Jr., by way of the Dixie Limited metaphor, points directly to Faulkner himself as the great power of the wilderness—the head bear, the Man, or the Chief ("Dixie Special" 37). For better and for worse, Isaac McCaslin has realized his true multiracial genealogy within the recreated landscape of the wilderness, much as his actual progenitor, William Faulkner, does. Thus railroads, for all of the biographical and textual continuities developed here, form one of the most important symbols of a complex cultural power dynamic involving geography and history as well as class, gender, and race in *Go Down, Moses*—and in many other works comprising Faulkner's canon.

As we have noted in chapter 2, Faulkner's biographical narratives reveal many images and symbols of tracks and trains, as we would anticipate from the scion of a railroad building family. The high modernist novels present fewer, though perhaps more symbolic, instances such as Quentin Compson's train and trolley rides in *The Sound and the Fury,* Vardaman Bundren's recollected toy train in the Jefferson shop window in *As I Lay Dying* (1930), and Temple Drake's ill-fated excursion in *Sanctuary,* which began when she jumps from a special train at the real station of Taylor a few miles below Oxford and concludes two decades later in *Requiem for a Nun.* The text most affected by its railroad imagery and symbolism is also the least modernist of this period, *Light in August* (1932), perhaps not surprisingly given its complications of gender, race, class. Trains thread their way both more realistically and comically through the later, more traditional fictions such as the Snopes trilogy: *The Hamlet* (1942), *The Town* (1957), and *The Mansion* (1959).

Outside of Yoknapatawpha, a distinction may be made between narratives using Northern and Western railroads and those employing European settings and railways. In America, *The Wild Palms* (1939) proves an important example as both its narrative sequences are rife with rail images and symbols from the North as well as the South that become significant in terms of gender. Beyond America, trains often figure in fictions of foreign travel, especially the war stories, in particular the allegorical novel appropriately titled *A Fable*. This epic tale makes particularly powerful use of tracks and trains, another aspect of this somewhat neglected and depreciated narrative that will repay closer and more sympathetic scrutiny than it has received recently from revisionist critics.

In conclusion, we might return again to Flannery O'Connor's anxious insight into both the literary power and the cultural limitations of William Faulkner's fiction. As a privileged white male, she tells us, Faulkner could view the South as if from the rear observation platform of the Dixie Limited, a commanding if still limiting viewpoint. O'Connor's metaphor may have been suggested by an allusion employed by Jean-Paul Sartre to explain Faulkner's modernist narrative technique: "As for Faulkner's heroes, they never foresee: the car takes them away, as they look back" (230). His reference is to *The Sound and the Fury*, to Quentin's train-ride home for the Christmas holiday during his fateful year at Harvard. Somewhere in Virginia, Quentin looks back at the figure of an older black man, sitting on a mule at a grade crossing, who reminds him of his family's retainer, Roskus. Sartre quotes the novel: "The train swung round the curve, the engine puffing short, heavy blasts, and they passed smoothly from sight that way" (*Sound* 106). So Quentin returns southward, his course determined by rails forged by men like Colonel William C. Falkner, toward the apocryphal country that formed him, much as actual history and geography formed his creator, William C. Faulkner.

With all deference to Sartre (after all none would believe one's little critical handcar could outrun the Train à Grande Vitesse), though Quentin did not change Faulkner certainly did, as we have seen in the transitions between chapters 2 and 4. Chapter 3 developed comparable changes in the earlier and later works of Thomas Wolfe, while chapters 5 and 8 will draw comparisons between Robert Penn Warren's earlier fiction, which proves indebted to the prodigious example of William Faulkner, and his later, postmodern poetry, which moves beyond the Fugitive/Agrarian traditions to become an example for a post-Southern generation of poets such as Dave Smith.

Chapter Five

Robert Penn Warren's Modern Fictive Railroads

All the King's Men and Others

The diner was built like a railway coach, but it was set on a concrete foundation in a lot just off the main street of town. At each end the concrete was painted to show wheels.

Robert Penn Warren,
The Circus in the Attic and Other Stories

1

Born on April 24, 1905, in the busy rail junction of Guthrie, Kentucky, Robert Penn Warren, like William Faulkner and Thomas Wolfe, came of age during the Golden Age of Southern railroading. As his works often recreate his life, especially his boyhood, they also reflect the importance of trains to the construction of the material culture and the imaginative vision of the South. Railroads reconstructed an earlier Dixie, from landscapes to time zones, from modes of perception to means of communication. For Warren, as for the other writers of the Southern Renaissance, trains represented not just efficient transportation and innovative technology but archetypal machines in traditional Southern gardens, and thus powerful symbols of cultural determinism in terms of gender, race, and class. Over the more than half a century separating Warren's earliest and latest writing, his formulations about and imagery of railroads provide an interesting and important index to his growth and development as both cultural critic and literary artist. Again like Faulkner and Wolfe, as we have seen in earlier chapters, Warren's images and symbols derived from the trains of his youth demonstrate a career-long dialogue engaging the other of gender, race, and class.

Although the increasing scholarly attention to Warren's literary achievement has considered railroad references within individual works, the persistence of this intriguing motif throughout his canon has yet to be traced. The present study relates railroads in Warren's life and work by consideration of both viewing and riding trains in his fiction and poetry, while regarding the locomotive as an artifact in Southern culture and a symbol in Southern literature. My reading will focus on his fiction in this chapter, because of its close connections to the novels of Faulkner and Wolfe, but will consider his poetry in chapter 8, because of its influence on more recent, postmodern efforts in that genre. In both early and later prose and poetry, Warren's recreated railroads encapsulate his most pervasive themes: the inexorable pull of place, the harsh determinations of time, and the precarious balance of the individual human identity in its relation to geography and history.

Warren's hometown owed its existence to the development of the rail network in Kentucky and Tennessee during Reconstruction; it was created by the crossing of trunk lines that became parts of the Louisville and Nashville Railroad, and it was named for Congressman James Guthrie, political sponsor and later president of this important railway system. The author's parents, Robert Franklin and Anna Ruth Penn Warren, married and moved to this lively little town in search of new opportunities only a year before his birth. In the years young Warren lived there, Guthrie was the stopping place of as many as twenty passenger trains a day, in addition to thirty or more freight and work trains. The railroad with its subsidiary crosstie plant became the area's leading employer, engendering a rapid growth and development that brought both frontier rowdiness and urban civilization to this raw town subdivided by both the L&N tracks and the border between Kentucky and Tennessee (Blotner *Warren* 5–7).

In several reminiscences of his youth in Guthrie, Warren remarks on this contrast of popular and literary cultures, one that later informs much of his writing. Warren recalls that the rough-and-tumble atmosphere of the rail yards and the creosote plant was not far removed from the respectable main street where his father worked and his mother shopped, or from the large railroad hotel with a newsstand where one could buy the metropolitan papers and the national magazines. As in most small towns of the railroad era, Guthrie's populace enjoyed visiting the railroad station, watching the trains, and noting the arrivals and departures of their passengers (*Portrait* 53–54). This excitement proved greatest for the crack express trains, like the prototype Dixie Limited, which suggested the glamorous aura of the larger world beyond the limitations of provincial Guthrie. In those early years of the century, the railroad was the only mode of long-distance travel, before either reliable automobiles or paved highways, so the only excitement greater than watching trains was actually riding them, experiencing directly the speed and power, the innovation and promise as yet unavailable in any other aspect of Southern culture.

2

Robert Penn Warren's prose fiction, in particular his novels, often make both realistic and symbolic use of railroads as they existed in this period about the turn of the twentieth century. For example, "Prime Leaf" (1931), Warren's first published short fiction, and *Night Rider* (1939), Warren's first published novel, provide his initial significant uses of railroad images, ones that prove both historically accurate and symbolically apt. Both of these narratives developed from the subject matter of the "Tobacco Wars," which in the early decades of the century ravaged Warren's region, the "Black Patch," the popular name given this dark-fired tobacco land in western Kentucky and Tennessee. These fierce power struggles pitted the larger growers demanding a greater share of the profits from the trade against the tobacco trusts bent on forcing down costs for their raw materials; their battles were determined and concluded as much by the region's railroads as by the shape and the use of the land itself. Although these rather important agricultural confrontations have been neglected somewhat by American historians, contemporary interest in struggles of class and race have led to their recent reconsideration. It proves interesting to note that these historical and economic reinterpretations corroborate Warren's creative rereading of the Black Patch War (Goff and Lile 1, Winn 68).

The subject matter of the Tobacco Wars resonated with geographical, historical, and biographical significance for Warren, who grew up during the struggle and saw it affect his own family, especially his maternal grandfather, Thomas Gabriel Penn, a Confederate cavalry officer, tobacco farmer and buyer, and a well-read, thoughtful man who became an important influence on his grandson. Most critical consideration of *Night Rider* concerns its relation to both historical models and sources, as well as to Warren's earlier and later writing, especially "Prime Leaf," which serves as a matrix for the novel (Shepherd 343–45). As with all of his works, Warren's titles prove significant: "prime leaf" is the cash crop of the dark-fired tobacco growers in the Black Patch, and it also becomes Warren's primary literary and textual commitment to his regional subjects.

The novella also proves intertextual with Warren's somewhat controversial essay on race and Southern culture, "The Briar Patch," first published in the Agrarian manifesto, *I'll Take My Stand* (1930). However, in "Prime Leaf," his subtle condemnation of segregation and sharecropping begins Warren's reconsideration of his traditional patria (Millichap 69–77). Set in the opening decade of the century, Warren's primal fiction uses railroads for both realistic and symbolic detail. His characters must take trains on any errand beyond a buggy ride, but as they travel they intertwine and develop as the plot crosses their paths at depots and junctions. For example, when old Joe Hardin takes the local accommodation to Bardsville for the tobacco growers meeting, he sees others differently, especially in the changed circumstances of the returning night train. In particular, one of the blacks on the station platform issues a premonitory blues moan in a call-and-response pattern with the departing locomotive; Joe notices, perhaps for the first time, "it was a deep and melancholy voice, full like the whistle" (*Circus* 241). By the time the author revises "Prime Leaf" as *Night Rider,* his criticism of Southern culture in terms of gender, race, and class is more direct, as his new title indicates.

Night Rider opens with the arrival of a crowded train carrying excited participants to the organizational rally of the tobacco farmers at Bardsville, a thinly disguised version of Guthrie, where just such an agricultural meeting was once attended by twenty-five thousand people (*Portrait* 53). The novel's protagonist, young lawyer/grower Perse Munn, comes more out of boredom than conviction, but he is soon impelled to a confused and finally tragic participation by the sheer momentum of the popular movement. These determinations begin with the crush of the crowd in the aisle of the braking train that forces Perse forward against his own will: "And as the movement of the crowd pushed him toward the door, Mr. Munn again resented that pressure that was human because it was made by human beings, but was inhuman, too, you could not isolate and blame any one of those human beings who made it" (*Night* 5).

Warren's opening scene serves as a microcosm of the novel's inevitable development, as his protagonist becomes dehumanized by participation in an association of growers and buyers who soon degenerate into an intimidating and increasingly violent gang of night riders. Although their most memorable nocturnal raids recall the tactics of Forrest's Confederate cavalry (in which both of Warren's grandfathers served, like the novel's Captain Todd and other characters) or the Ku Klux Klan, which Forrest also commanded (and in which both the same characters and their historical models may have participated), larger strategies are dictated by the centrality of railroads, again much like the final outcomes of the Civil War and Reconstruction, as argued in chapter 1. Fictive Bardsville, like historical Guthrie, became the site of the dark-fired tobacco growers' rally because of its convenience as a rail junction. The larger economic struggle is centered symbolically at the railheads, where the trusts' monopoly power is ranged against the growers' monopsony power (Goff and Lile 1).

The passage of the evening train determines and signals the night riders' boldest raid on the Bardsville buildings held by the tobacco trusts (*Night* 116). More importantly, the railroads also decide the conflict by bringing trainloads of troops to restore order after the destruction of the bulging warehouses. Although some die-hards take to the hills, burning individual barns and homes, their fate is determined at the moment the steaming engine pulls the troop train into Bardsville's depot, an apt symbol of the larger economic and political interests that determine and direct modern Southern life. "At last, flecking off steam like spittle, roaring and grinding on the polished steel of the rails, shaking the boards of the platform with the vibrations of its mass, scattering the pigeons in a crazy, tumultuous flock, the locomotive pulled past" (*Night* 154). At the novel's conclusion, the protagonist watches the orderly movement of the daily trains from his hiding place in the woods (*Night* 268), and the railroads become reiterated symbols of the farmers' failure to slow the commercial power of the trusts—as well as of the cultural and social forces that hem in Perse Munn, and the psychological and personal confusions that eventuate in his inevitable destruction.

3

By contrast, viewing the world from the window of a passing train provides a different symbolic viewpoint on both geography and history for the destabilized self in Warren's fictional masterpiece, *All the King's Men* (1946). Here the faintly autobiographical protagonist, Jack Burden, uses a slow journey on a branch-line accommodation train to define himself in relation to place, time, and self. Jack crosses the cut-over pine woods of his unnamed native state to report on the rally at Upton during Willie Stark's first, unsuccessful campaign for governor. Until this rural rally, Willie is exploited by the city political machine in order to split the "cocklebur" vote, much as Jack is exploited by his urban newspaper to slant his reporting in favor of the city boss. The rally proves a turning point in both characters' development, and Jack's metaphysical train journey provides not only the impetus for these events but also their interpretation by him.

In a scene intertextual with Thomas Wolfe, Warren lets his protagonist view the changing landscapes through the day-coach window like a historical panorama, one that becomes representative of his personal as well as regional history. Jack watches a slattern pitch a dish pan of dirty water from a back porch by the tracks and then retreat into the inviolable secrecy of her shack. His reaction becomes more psychological than sociological: "And all at once, you think that you are the one who is running away, and who better run fast to wherever you are going because it will be dark soon" (*All* 76). When he sees a bucolic evening scene beyond the ramshackle town, his confidence is not restored by the despoiled landscape: "And all at once you feel like crying" (76). Jack's idle tears are motivated by cultural and personal history, evoked by the rapid juxtaposition of the scenes by the train, which in so doing replicates the historical extension of civilized discontents into the innocence of nature.

Earlier in the novel (though recalled and not directly narrated), during a trip to Willie Stark's home place in these same red hills, Jack employs the railroad as a symbol of the economic and environmental exploitation that wasted this country and its people: "The bastards got in here and set up the mills and laid the narrow-gauge tracks and knocked together the company commissaries . . . till, all of a sudden, there weren't any more pine trees" (2). Warren's mechanical images recall William Faulkner's in *Go Down, Moses,* where the narrow-gauge railroad becomes a snake violating the Edenic big woods, until then the preserve of primitive hunters or adept sportsmen.

At the same time, something more personal and psychological probably is present here as well, since Jack has been separated from his heritage by the wealth generated in these same sorts of exploitations, a condition most obvious in his failed relationships and lonely travels. In another passage of almost metaphysical complexity, Jack images the coming of darkness and sleep in terms of a small boy anxiously waiting for a passenger train. "You get so you listen for night . . . long before it comes charging and stewing and thundering to you like a big black locomotive and the black cars grind to a momentary stop and the porter with the black, shining face helps you up the steps, and says, 'Yassuh, little boss, yassuh'" (100). The positioning of this passage proves most important, as Jack recounts how he becomes a "little boss" for Willie, the "Big Boss," by way of his strained relations with his parents, his failed loves and marriage, and his uncompleted doctoral dissertation on the subject of his familial forbear, Cass Mastern, another sensitive young man destroyed by the dark and complicated history of black bondage and its ensuing cultural determinations.

So trains mark Jack's failures, which he flees in his "Great Sleeps," near suicidal fugues that reinforce his incomplete devel-

opment and are connected with train images. Jack's putative father, the so-called Scholarly Attorney, makes a legal errand to an
Arkansas Delta lumber town and meets the beautiful and ambitious young woman who will become Jack's mother; they start
back to Burden's Landing by way of the same railroad that created the lumber camp and the need for timber litigation (129).
His parents' divorce evidently affects Jack's relationships negatively, especially with Anne Stanton; his failure to consummate
their young love is punctuated by the haunting whistle of the
11:45 train into Burden's Landing that signals the nightly conclusion to their trysts (276). Of course, the interpolated Mastern
episode presents several instances of race and railroads, especially the relation of brothers Cass (who ignores railroads and
frees slaves) and Gilbert (who buys slaves and builds railroads),
which also parallels the pairing of Jack and Willie and that of
Ike McCaslin and Cass Edmonds in Faulkner's *Go Down, Moses*
(*All* 216). Finally, it is a train ride to Savannah, reversing Cass's
journeying, which starts Jack on the road to the truth of his paternity, the plot's ultimate revelation (160).

   All the King's Men consistently has received the most extensive critical attention among Warren's works, especially with a
resurgence of interest at its fiftieth anniversary in 1996. Not all
of this consideration has proved positive, however, as Warren has
been recently reassessed by revisionist critics in terms of an alleged disengagement with race, gender, and class. For example,
Forrest G. Robinson's study, "A Combat with the Past: Robert
Penn Warren on Race and Slavery" (1995), provides a specula-
tive reconsideration of *All the King's Men,* if not an entirely con-
vincing one, by positing a failure to directly address Southern
racial problems in the 1930s. Warren had already defended himself by pointing out that blacks did not play a major role in the
Depression-era politics of the Deep South and by including the
interpolated Cass Mastern exemplum to foreground the racial
themes. Although Robinson raises interesting questions about
the novel, his revision of Warren, like a good deal of politically
correct criticism of traditional canonical figures of the Southern
Renaissance practiced recently, often misses the ways in which
all of them—especially Faulkner, Wolfe, and Warren—are constantly engaged in active dialogue with the "others" of gender,

race, and class, at least subtly and indirectly (and often overtly and directly), especially in their later works.

Robinson's article goes backward in time from *All the King's Men* to reflexively fault Warren for his retrograde racial stance in "The Briar Patch" (1930), though the essay was published sixteen years earlier when the author was twenty-five years old. Robinson acknowledges but discounts Warren's remarks in 1957 about writing his way out of the essay in fiction; the critic makes no mention, however, of the works Warren directly addressed in this context, "Prime Leaf" and *Night Rider.* Robinson's argument also overlooks the republication of "Prime Leaf" as the final selection in *The Circus in the Attic* (1947), Warren's only short-fiction sequence, which serves as a sort of gloss on his greatest novel published a year earlier (Millichap 3–8). Finally, for whatever reasons, Robinson ignores the greater portion of Warren's later fiction, almost all of his nonfiction in the 1960s and 1970s, much of it directly addressing the national crisis of race, nearly all of his literary criticism, and all of his poetry, which earned him two Pulitzer prizes and the first national laureateship and in which he reinscribed his relation to his place and time.

4

The Circus in the Attic and Other Stories is Robert Penn Warren's only work in a genre used by several important writers in the modern era, notably William Faulkner in *Go Down, Moses.* Like Faulkner's volume, Warren's collects a number of "twice-told tales," rearranges several, and develops one, the title novella, to make it serve as an introduction for the overall narrative. Although not as tightly unified as Faulkner's sequence, Warren's narrative involves similar characters, events, and settings: for the most part middle-class Southern white males from Warren's homeland are initiated into the frustrations and failures of relationships with others (Millichap 8). "Prime Leaf" set this pattern early in Warren's career, and he uses it as one bookend for his grouping. The other is the title novella, whose intriguing title image provides a matrix for the entire cycle of narratives.

In "Circus in the Attic," Bolton Lovehart, the symbolically named protagonist, constructs a model circus as a small world he can control, in contrast to the larger worlds of Bardsville and Carruthers County, whose history he is supposed to be writing. Warren loosely based his story on a reclusive eccentric from Hopkinsville, Kentucky, but the imagery becomes faintly auto-biographical as well, for the toy circus evolves as an elaborate trope for the creative process, as in Thomas Wolfe's image of the tiny circus as avant-garde art. Bardsville's typical Southern culture proves a sort of historical three-ring circus, while Bolton becomes its clown, not its ringmaster, in his relation to a set of female figures suggesting the attractive acrobat of his dreams.

Railroads figure as both realistic detail and symbolic structuring, as the traditional circus of Warren's era traveled by special train. The narrative voice opens the novella and the volume with a detailed description of Bardsville, and its railroad infrastructure is highlighted: "The tracks, switches, and sidings [were] exposed among the jumble, like a tangle of dissected nerves, to glitter, too, and quiver in the incandescent light" (*Circus* 3). In this area and era, the rail lines are like the nervous system of the changing Southern culture, as we have seen in earlier works by Warren, Wolfe, and Faulkner. When Bolton is twelve, he tries to escape his smothering mother by running off on the circus train, only to be tracked by his distant father to the Memphis railroad yards and returned to his colorless life in Bardsville. After that abortive chase after a more colorful life, our protagonist's only trains will be the models that transport the toy circus he secretly constructs in his locked attic study.

Although railroads appear as both realistic and symbolic detail in several narratives between the bookend novellas, the most interesting instance is another toy train in Warren's best-known story, "Blackberry Winter." Seth, the ten-year-old white protagonist, plays with his black counterpart's homemade toy train: "Old Jebb had put spool wheels on three cigar boxes and put wire links between the boxes to make a train for Jebb" (80). In this well-known initiation tale, Seth must come to terms with otherness through a succession of symbolic figures ranging from his own mother and father, to his friend's older parents, to the desperate white tramp who haunts their home place on this unseasonably cold June day in 1910. The little train becomes a symbolic text, like the toy circus, with its load of "colored rocks, and fossils of crinoid stems, and other stuff" (80). Seth's narration is filled with all the "stuff" of a changing Southern culture, especially the trains that brought the world-weary tramp to them from the city and will carry off the black shadow family from the homeland to the city in the future.

Interestingly enough, Warren's last published novel, *A Place to Come To* (1977), employs similar railroad images over three decades after his single masterpiece and well into the postmodern period. Here another slightly autobiographical protagonist, Jed Tewksbury, tries to find his way home again after leaving Dugtown, Alabama, for a career as a classical scholar. Again, trains represent the historical dimensions of his sojourns, just as they determined the Southern mill town that spawned him. Jed takes the train to the state college, to graduate school at the University of Chicago, to service in the Second World War—which sends him behind enemy lines in Italy—then back to graduate school supported by the G.I. Bill and an early marriage. After his wife's untimely death, Jed makes his first attempt at repatriation by taking an assistant professorship at Vanderbilt in 1951. Indeed, he rides the night streamliner from Chicago to Nashville, a train much like the Dixie Limited, which would have stopped at Guthrie even in these postwar years of passenger service cutbacks.

Jed spends the evening at the bar in the lounge car, idly talking with a lubricious female passenger, his first flirtation since the death of his young wife over a year before. Like Perse Munn in the first novel, these "night riders" are impelled toward a lost future, in this case encouraged both by the isolation of the speeding train and the impersonal and ironic ministrations of the "black barman" (*Place* 119). At this juncture, Jed still resists a relationship, even one as casual as that suggested by his traveling companion's offer of a "nightcap" in her personal compartment (120). Later Jed contemplates the stormy dark rushing past his own Pullman window, a perspective that propels him toward a deterministic view of his life and the human condition.

The memory of his dead wife, whom he knows he never really loved, leaves him "only with a grinding pain and a vision of the way the world was" (121). One part of how the world is becomes imaged in the fantasy of his drinking companion also masturbating in her lonely cubicle, a prefiguring of Jed's kinky reunion in Tennessee with his first love, the lovely though lost Rozelle Hardcastle. Unlike Perse Munn, however, Jed Tewksbury is able to resist and even ride the motion of history. Along his way, he encounters other railroads and trains both in America and in Europe, where he returns after the war. Jed's travels finally turn toward some sort of reconciliation with his widowed stepfather, the good old boy Perk Simms back in Dugtown—and toward a more hopeful philosophy of time, history, and the individual self.

Other interesting Warren fictions referencing railroads include "The Apple Tree" and "God's Own Time," early unpublished novels set in small towns much like Guthrie with much time spent around the tracks; *At Heaven's Gate* (1943), which contrasts trains with automobiles and airplanes, as in *All the King's Men;* and *Band of Angels* (1955), which follows the railroads to the Western frontier following the Civil War. So Robert Penn Warren's voluminous canon contains many interesting examples of railroad imagery and symbolism that function as an important index to his most pervasive ideas and themes. Again, these examples extend from his earliest efforts in fiction, especially *Night Rider,* his first published novel, to his masterpiece, *All the King's Men,* to his final novel, *A Place to Come To.* Warren's short fiction and nonfiction prose often presents railroad images important for their biographical references and cultural commentary as well. However, Warren's later poems, certainly more personal and perhaps even more penetrating than his prose, reveal the pervading patterns of railroads as image and idea, as we will see in chapter 8. All of these works, considered both individually and collectively, corroborate the pervasive themes of place's inexorable pull, time's dark determinations, and the self's precarious positioning in relation to both geography and history, and by extension to considerations of gender, race, and class, themes most often discovered in Robert Penn Warren's real and recreated railroads.

Chapter Six

Eudora Welty's Real and Recreated Railroads

Delta Wedding

After dinner in the sparkling dining car, my father and I walked back to the open-air observation platform at the end of the train and sat on the folding chairs placed at the railing. We watched the sparks we made fly behind us in the night.

Eudora Welty, *One Writer's Beginnings*

1

As indicated in chapter 1, a railroad map of America in 1861 not only symbolizes why the South lost the Civil War but also suggests how trains became such an important aspect of postbellum Southern culture. In addition to the railroad's archetypal symbolism as the machinery of the twentieth century transfiguring the traditional Southern garden, regional history also freighted the train with special import as a cultural marker. Like many other aspects of its heritage, the Old South's cavalier attitudes toward railroads were transformed by the trauma of the Civil War and Reconstruction into the New South's faith in tracks and trains, so that the completion of the Southern railway network signaled Dixie's cultural resurgence in the twentieth century. In turn, writing in the South inscribed this ambivalent relation to railroads, so that tracks and trains became important tropes in the Southern Renaissance, as we have already seen.

Most of the writers who produced this renaissance of Southern letters were born about the turn of the century and came to maturity during the Golden Age of Southern railroading. The most obvious examples include canonical figures, such as the subjects of earlier chapters—William Faulkner, Thomas Wolfe, and Robert Penn Warren—all of whom employ extensive railroad references in contrasting tradition and modernity. In the African American literature of the South, trains reached an almost mythic status as a major means of the Great Migration; this ambiguous symbolism of determinism and freedom extends from blues and gospel lyrics to their reiteration in literary works by writers such as Jean Toomer, Langston Hughes, Richard Wright and Ralph Ellison—as I will demonstrate in chapter 7. Women authors as different as Zora Neale Hurston, Caroline Gorden, Katherine Anne Porter, Margaret Mitchell, Carson McCullers, and Flannery O'Connor also recreate Southern railroads in their reconfigurations of regional history. Among women writers of the South, the most distinctive use of trains is discovered in Eudora Welty's real and recreated railroads, especially in *Delta Wedding* (1946), where the cultural importance of the actual railroads Welty represents adds meaning to her structural use of this controlling metaphor within the cultural traditions of the Southern Renaissance.

Born in 1909, Eudora Welty grew up in Jackson, Mississippi's capital and the hub of the Commonwealth's rail network, then at its greatest expansion. Railroad imagery pervades her autobiographical writing as much as her fiction, in particular *One Writer's Beginnings* (1984), indicating a personal and an intellectual interest in trains inculcated by her father. Railroads provide realistic detail in her fiction, but they also become important symbolic markers that represent the structural changes transforming the Magnolia State along with the rest of the South. Examples are found across her career, including stories such as "Lily Daw and the Three Ladies" (1941), "The Bride of Innisfallen" (1955), and "The Demonstrators" (1980), as well as longer fictions such as *The Ponder Heart* (1954), *Losing Battles* (1970), and *The Optimist's Daughter* (1972). Given her widespread use of trains, surprisingly few of Welty's critics have considered this pattern, though it connects her with other writers of the Southern Renaissance (Gretlund 159, 212).

Many critics of *Delta Wedding* have recognized the importance of railroads to Welty's narrative structure, and some have remarked that her fictional examples are drawn from actual proto-types (Gretlund 254–55). No reader, however, as yet combines her real and recreated trains in a cultural reading of the novel. An innovative approach seems especially important as her first novel proves a pivotal work in Welty's canon, poised as it is between the earlier, shorter fictions that established her critical reputation and the later, longer works that confirmed her popular acceptance. To some extent, this popular success responds to changes in theme, tone, and mode as Eudora Welty moved from the dark naturalism of many stories to the comic realism of the novels.

The complicated development of *Delta Wedding* confirms its transitional position in the Welty canon. The narrative began as a short story, "Delta Cousins," which evolved from a complex matrix of memory and invention. Welty evidently began her story as a series of sketches in letters to her Jackson friend, John Robinson, who was then serving with the armed forces in Europe. The writer's recreation of Delta life between the world wars combined her own occasional observations and Robinson's reminiscences of his extended family in the Delta crossroads of Sidon, Mississippi. Welty's "Delta Cousins" ordered these materials through the viewpoint of a young girl from Jackson visiting her country relations, adding a faint autobiographical stance to the narrative and allowing the writer to filter these scenes through her own imagination.

Developing the story as a novel was suggested by her agent, Diarmuid Russell, who intuited greater possibilities for the material. Welty's additions seem to be largely her inventions, including several key elements that project a more complicated view of regional geography and history. Since its first reviewers, critics of the novel have been divided in their conception of its fictive stance in relation to Southern culture, in particular its recreation of Southern attitudes on the vexed triad of gender, class, and race. Somewhat simply put, some critics, especially early reviewers, find the narrative a realistic Southern novel marred by nostalgia for a patriarchal garden, while others, especially recent feminist scholars, feel the book is a delightful Southern romance, marked by a delineation of a matriarchal paradise. My reading of *Delta Wedding* will use Welty's actual and imagined railroads to delineate an ambivalent narrative tension between the geographical and historical reality of the South and its cultural myth as represented by the history and culture of the Mississippi Delta.

Railroads, especially in their Southern incarnations, were until quite recently masculine, white, and middle- or upper-class—in a word, patriarchal—in their conception, operation, and appreciation; women, blacks, and the working class were relegated to supporting, demeaning, and secondary roles. As we have seen, serious Southern literature has used trains to represent these imbalances of cultural power, particularly in their material determinations; other writers of the Southern Renaissance share in such railroad imagery—for example, William Faulkner in fictions such as "Delta Autumn," a work in several ways intertextual with *Delta Wedding* both in its railroad images and in other patterns, as we have seen in chapter 4. It is also interesting to observe how female, black, and working-class writers adapt and innovate these symbolic patterns and practices in their extension of the Southern Renaissance. Welty becomes a particularly interesting example, as she uses real and recreated trains both extensively and intensively in her writing.

2

As if in demonstration of its structural importance, Welty opens *Delta Wedding* with a train. "The nickname of the train was the Yellow Dog. Its real name was the Yazoo-Delta. It was a mixed train" (*Delta* 3). At the most basic levels of narrative, Welty's Yellow Dog is both a realistic and a striking detail, as its colorful name is both historically accurate and an apt device of plot development. The train journey shapes the experience of her surrogate, nine-year-old Laura McRaven, by bringing her from Jackson into the very different world of the Delta. The long opening in the whites-only coach of the local accommodation train introduces character, initiates plot, establishes setting, and reveals the imaginative tone of Welty's narrative in several ways. Most important is the sense of immersion in paradisiacal nature, as the train dips from the trunk line along the upland ridge onto the branch line that descends into the Delta itself. Traveling toward the sunset, the train, like everything else in this rich land, is suffused by a glow highlighted in the autumnal blossoms, the yellow butterflies, and the "dark gold and shadowy . . . river, the Yazoo"; even Laura's destination, the tiny station at Fairchilds, is "the dark-yellow color of goldenrod" (5). Welty critics have reacted both positively and negatively to this mythic sense of a golden time in a golden land, a seemingly maternal welcome for little Laura, who only recently has lost her own mother, Annie Laurie Fairchild McRaven, to a shadowy illness. The positive reading of the landscape is made by feminist critics, though the early death of the romantically named young mother vitiates any sense of rosy nostalgia in Laura's journey toward maturity.

At the same time, little Laura's arrival suggests something of the modern machine penetrating this traditional Delta garden. Although the unlighted lamp in the coach is decorated in a pattern of floral cutouts, its "kerosene smell" is still discernible. When Laura stretches her arm into the golden sunlight it is sprinkled with the smokestack's "soot," while in the darkening fields she watches "Delta buzzards" wheeling above a "black mule" and the "fading train of dust" its movement creates(4). Her closest traveling companion, a traveling salesman across the aisle, with his ticket stuck in the band of his straw hat, groans and sinks into sleep as the Yellow Dog rambles deeper into the Delta. Railroads like this one are the technological connections to the larger world, the commercial links that make the extractive industry and plantation economy viable here. Despite the natural, even feminine imagery associated with the Yellow Dog, the whistle-stop town of Fairchilds, and Shellmound plantation, the characters' references to the feeder rail line reinforce this masculine sense of a commercial link. The mixed trains carry out the raw lumber and cotton and cart back the finished goods that will be used to construct the cultural community, much as in Faulkner's "Delta Autumn." The materials that will complement this Delta wedding become prime examples: hothouse flowers, spun-sugar cakes, and shepherdess crooks for the bridesmaids in the Arcadian fantasy (Hardy 397).

Another symbolic scene involving the Yellow Dog invokes this darker side of the railroad. Almost as soon as she arrives at Shellmound, Laura is told about the near "tragedy" (19), two weeks earlier, when a family fishing party was overtaken by the local train on the Dry Creek trestle. Her mentally limited Cousin Maureen caught her foot between the cross ties (or perhaps pretended to), and her beloved, heroic Uncle George Fairchild put himself at risk trying to free her. Fortunately the train was able to stop short of them, despite the inattention of its engineer, Mr. Doolittle, and the incident ended as comedy when both uncle and niece comically tumbled from the tracks and facetious apologies were extended all around. This Disney-like incident is not dramatized but presented through the varied recollections and reactions of all the characters. The first retelling is by fourteen-year-old Orrin in the manner of the novel itself, "like narrations, chronological and careful" (20), thus establishing the details that will be interpreted by each of the characters according to their own needs; for example, Laura states "gravely," shyly, and much in character, "I'm glad I wasn't there" (30).

The reactions of others prove more complex, both emotionally and intellectually. The strongest emotions are evidently stirred in Dabney Fairchild, the nubile, seventeen-year-old daughter of the family, and Troy Flavin, the Fairchild's manly, if hillborn, overseer; though they have been sweethearts but a short time and despite the fact that he is twice her age, they make up their minds to wed quickly, thus raising eyebrows all around. At the other extreme of emotional reaction is Robbie Reid Fairchild, George's young, perhaps pregnant wife, who resents her husband's risking himself for any one other than herself; she decides to leave George, their home in Memphis, and the Fairchild family for her own people, the shopkeeping Reid clan. Likewise more emotional than thoughtful are India and Shelley Fairchild, Dabney's younger and older sisters; India characteristically wishes to exaggerate the incident, while Shelley is frustrated that she did not rise to the occasion. Several characters impatiently dismiss the whole affair, such as the dim Shellmound patriarch, Battle Fairchild, and his sister, Tempe Fairchild Summers, the matriarch of Inverness plantation.

The most ambivalent reactions are those of George himself and of his sister-in-law, Ellen Dabney Fairchild, the mistress of Shellmound. George Fairchild is the central character of the narrative, at least in a symbolic sense, much as the confrontation on

Dry Creek trestle proves the central symbolic event of the plot. Just as she never fully reveals this central scene, Welty never takes George's point of view on it or on anything else, perhaps because George seems a variation of the archetypal male principle. Although not yet a patriarch, he is a warrior who is "wounded" as a glamorous "aeronaut" (25, 134). Welty's reference to her male character as a wounded airman restless at home and mourning a dead brother after the Great War seems intertextual to William Faulkner and his fictive surrogates in autobiographical family sagas like *Sartoris* and *Flags in the Dust,* works equally rich in train images because of his family's historical involvement with railroad building in northern Mississippi. George's understanding of his brush with fate on the railroad trestle proves instinctive, assertive, and stoical; he does what he must do, and he accepts it philosophically. As he finally puts it to Robbie in their reconciliation scene, "I don't think it matters what *happens* to a person, or what comes. . . . Something is always coming you know that" (187, emphasis in original).

At the opposite extreme, Welty gives Ellen the most important viewpoint in the narrative, as the wedding she orchestrates becomes the most important narrated event. In many ways, Ellen is the most thoughtful and insightful of all the characters, though, like her younger niece Laura, she is still an outsider in the family, two decades and eight children after her arrival as a young bride from the Virginia hills. Ellen, now in her tenth pregnancy, demonstrates an archetypal feminine indulgence in her relationship with George. Ellen knows the Fairchilds will reduce the incident at the Dry Creek trestle to a "romantic and absurd" family legend (188), but her viewpoint develops the human complexities involved. Her reactions range from the realistic, to the emotional, and, finally, to the philosophical: "It was *inevitable* that George . . . should stand on the trestle—on the track where people could be killed, thrown with their beauty disfigured before strangers into the blackberry bushes" (221, emphasis in original).

3

Finally, Ellen alone understands the full import of the events at the trestle, and through her guilty knowledge, she feels the conflicted symbolism of the railroads. Another character, one known only by George and Ellen, is obliterated by another train in the course of Welty's narrative, and her tragic fate reveals the dark underside of the Fairchild dream world. On an errand before the wedding, Ellen meets a ragged runaway girl in the depths of the woods near the bayou, a young person she naturally associates with her own daughters. On a mythic level, this striking young woman seems almost a spirit, like the female ghost said to haunt the bayou or a dryad of this narrow, dense forest. In her preoccupation with her own daughter's wedding, Ellen points the girl toward Memphis, "the old Delta synonym for pleasure, trouble, and shame" (72), though she instinctively regrets her indifference and self-absorption. Later, Ellen imparts her vision to Battle, who complains at his wife for crossing the bayou without a pistol, and to George, who remarks matter-of-factly that he seduced the runaway in the abandoned Argyle cotton gin—both obviously deficient, if patriarchal, even phallocentric, reactions.

George's casual, perhaps cynical remark surprises both Ellen and the reader. Although given to impulse, George's other impulsive actions seem positive, even protective of others, including Shellmound's women and children, both white and black. Even if he is only fantasizing about his relation with the mystery girl to flirt with Ellen in reaction to Robbie's flight, his words suggest the constant threat to gender polity that characterizes Welty's fiction. Also, the novel's consistent references to firearms belie the peaceful conception of the plantation, since, as with other engines of destruction, they provide a parallel and supporting pattern for the ambivalent imagery of trains. In particular, consider the heroic description of the Shellmound's stock of arms spread throughout the living room (119–20). Although most of these weapons are connected with the Fairchild men, several are associated with the Shellmound women, interestingly enough, again by the plantation's men.

After the ceremony the city photographer, down to record the wedding for the Memphis paper, mentions a gruesome picture already in his satchel and probably fated for publication in that tabloid. "Train victim. I got a girl killed on the I.C. Railroad. My train did it. Ladies, she was flung off in the blackberry bushes. Looked to me like she was walking up the track to Memphis and met Number 3" (218). The camera flash reveals "a vision of fate" to Ellen: "Surely this was the young girl of the bayou woods that was the victim this man had seen" (218). The awful fate of the unfortunate young woman, the darkest event in the narrative, becomes the nexus of many of the novel's symbols and modes. For example, the photographs of the artificially posed wedding party are contrasted with the corpse awkwardly tossed in the briar patch. (Surely, the photographer means that he has an image of the waif in his "portmanteau," not her mangled corpse, as Patricia Yaeger seems to imply in her effort to uncover grotesquerie in Welty's fiction [58–59]). Thus, photographic images introduce another technology of the nineteenth century changing in the twentieth century.

Because of Welty's lifelong interest in photography, critics have given considerable attention to relationships between her photography and her fiction, especially in terms of her early pictures for the Works Progress Administration in the 1930s and her first stories (Marrs 280; Weston, "Images" 80). In one sense, the two pictures contrasted here in *Delta Wedding* reflect the contrasting modes of her earlier (shorter) and later (longer) fictions: the snapshot revealing a single character in a flash of insight, and the more carefully composed group portrait exposing the relation of the characters within the larger scene. Of course, the tragic and comic subject matters of the two photographs prove even more important here.

Not only does this vision reveal the nightmare possibilities inherent in the dreamlike trestle incident, it underlines the narrative's delicate balance of Southern history and legend. The fatal track must be the main line of the Illinois Central, Mississippi's first and still most important railroad between Memphis and Jackson, while train number 3 is the "I.C. Special," the express between Chicago and New Orleans. The Illinois Central has other historical and legendary connections in Mississippi as well. On April 29, 1900, John Luther "Casey" Jones died in a wreck of the Chicago Fast Mail, an earlier incarnation of the I.C. Special at Vaughan, Mississippi; his black "engine wiper" created the ballad that made Casey Jones eponymous after it was appropriated by white vaudevillians (Hansen 34). Although some 2,500 railroad workers were killed that millennial

year, the legend of Casey Jones was built on his last-second hero-
ics in trying to save his train: ironically, the "brave engineer" in
all probability caused the wreck, as the fatigue of a second straight
ten-hour shift at the throttle made him miss a signal (Hansen
36). A later incarnation of the I.C. Special was named The City of
New Orleans, and Steve Goodman's elegiac ballad of the same
title (1970), covered by many contemporary folk, country, and
rock figures, made the train the best known in contemporary rail
lore while marking the end of the line for one romantic vision of
the railroad.

In *Delta Wedding,* the dark reality of the railroad in the
Southern landscape becomes obvious as this modern machine
penetrates the Southern garden of tradition. Unlike the Yellow
Dog, this main-line train will not pause in its rush for a stray
waif on its track, and the arresting image likewise comments on
the problematics of gender, race, and class in Welty's vision. Neither patriarchal power nor matriarchal care preserves this poor
girl, though as Ellen notes her "skin was white to transparency"
(70). The Fairchilds' golden land and time is sustained by sacri-
fices like this one, though most often the scapegoats are
Shellmound's black residents, silently working to support this complex domestic scene. For example, the distracted black servant girl,
Pinchy, is associated with the lost white girl, as Ellen first assumed
it was the black adolescent, seemingly on some sort of religious
and/or sexual quest, who was hiding in the woods (Ladd 541).

Also, Aunt Studney, "coal-black, old as the hills," wanders
the "railroad track anywhere between Greenwood and Clarksdale"
(173), carrying an enigmatic dark sack that the Fairchild children associate with their mother's many babies (Moore 596). Aunt
Studney also provides a link between modern horrors and more
traditional terrors seen at deserted Marmion, the rather Gothic
plantation house across the Yazoo, visited by Laura and Cousin
Roy. The romantically named mansion was the first Fairchild
seat, and though it will pass eventually to Laura through her
mother's will, Dabney and Troy will live in it after their honey-
moon. The strange, dreamlike visit by the youngsters directly
before the wedding seems like some sort of weird initiation, one
that bodes ill for a bright future for any of those involved with
this location (Weston *Gothic* 94).

4

Aunt Studney's path could be by way of the I.C. main line, where one waif was lost, or the secondary Yellow Dog route, where another was saved. This contrast reminds the reader that Welty's branch line, virtually the Fairchild's garden railway in their view, was an actual "common carrier." By 1923, the feeder line was part of the Yazoo and Mississippi Valley, a regional carrier that had absorbed an earlier logging line named the Yazoo Delta, yielding the Y.D. initials interpreted by Delta blacks as the Yellow Dog. The term itself is also associated with cowardice, fever, mud, labor contracts, party-line politics in the South (i.e., "Yellow Dog Democrats"), and other topics that might provide a cultural interpretation of the Y.D. initials. The actual Yellow Dog train was a local freight boarded without fare by Delta "riders"; the corresponding through freight on the Illinois Central was called the "High Brown," evidently because only more daring African Americans would chance jumping it at speed for the faster trip to Memphis (Botkin and Harlow 499–500).

Eudora Welty's Yellow Dog is presented as a "mixed train," one mixing freight and passenger cars but also with symbolic, separate coaches for "white" and "colored" passengers (235). Other modes of transportation also demonstrate cultural constructions as well. The planters drive automobiles, while their hands ride on or behind horses and mules. At least the Fairchild women have their own horses and autos; in fact, Dabney receives both a walking horse and a Pierce-Arrow as wedding presents from her uncles, George and Pinckney. The wedding couple rides the train to New Orleans and observes a streetcar named "Desire" (245), long before Tennessee Williams's play (1947) made it even more remarkable. Shelly even goes as far as racing the Fairchild Studebaker against the Yellow Dog, though its male engineer stops his train with patronizing Southern male gallantry, seeming to let her win (235).

The Yellow Dog, long since absorbed by the Illinois Central and later abandoned, cross-stitched the homeland of the Delta blues, and was immortalized in W.C. Handy's "Yellow Dog Blues" (1914) and by many other classic blues lyrics. Stranded at a rail junction, Handy heard a local blues man singing in Moorhead,

Mississippi—the crossroads of the Delta where the rails of the Columbus and Greenville, a Southern Railway subsidiary, and the Yazoo and Mississippi Valley, by then an Illinois Central subsidiary, crossed on a level grade. This junction in time became a legendary locus of Delta blues, so that even in Chicago juke joints deracinated or exiled Mississippi bluesmen would identify each other by asking who knew where the "Southern cross de Dog." In his popular history of the Delta, Frank E. Smith retells the Yellow Dog tale, includes the lyrics of W.C. Handy's "Yellow Dog Blues," and points out that the infamous Mississippi State Prison Farm at Parchman was also on the Yellow Dog route. As the train for visitors from Jackson did not arrive until late evening, the railroad also gave rise to the famous blues ballad "Midnight Special," transposed by Huddie "Leadbelly" Ledbetter and other blues artists to varied prison settings across the South.

Although Welty is very precise about her chronological setting in September 1923, chosen because no great historical events would distract her characters (Bunting 721), she is less so about the locations in the novel. Fairchilds and Shellmound are fictitious, of course, though there is a place called Shellmound, the site of an Indian mound comprised of mussel shells, near Greenwood, Mississippi. In any case, Shellmound is in the "Yellow Dog District," with Greenwood as its market town and close enough to Parchman to hear the sirens when a prisoner escaped. This general area also includes James Robinson's family home in Sidon, Mississippi. However, its proximity to the Yazoo River becomes a problem, as Welty's railroad runs on the wrong bank. In her original treatment of the material in the story "Delta Cousins," the river is the Sunflower, so the relation with the railroad is correct. The Choctaw/Chickasaw name Yazoo is generally interpreted as meaning the "River of Death," from a battle at Shellmound that cost the allied tribes many casualties. In writing her novel, it seems likely that Welty changed the names of her rivers for thematic purposes but neglected to switch railroads and river banks.

5

Shellmound's black men with symbolic names and matching qualities, like the injured Big Baby, the restless Man-Son, and the rebellious Root M'Hook, suggest the heritage of African American bluesmen, the disaffected poets of the Great Migration (Ferris 20). In *Delta Wedding,* the potentially deadly confrontation between Root and Troy, the black man armed with an ice pick and the white man armed with a pistol, leaves the worker wounded and the overseer late for his rehearsal dinner, another deft contrast between the dark realities of the Fairchild hegemony and the bright celebration of its cultural continuities in this Delta wedding.

Welty again seems to be reconfiguring Faulkner, whose most recent publication was *Go Down, Moses* (1942), which appeared only a few years before the composition of *Delta Wedding;* both books present Delta settings, similar down to the contrasted Indian mounds and railroad embankments, the racial confrontations in plantation commissaries, and the sacrificial imagery drawn from the Old Testament. Finally, Faulkner's view of the Delta is more tragically determined, Welty's more comically ambivalent. Even the symbolic castration of Root M'Hook, whose index finger is bloodied in the exchange, is comically undercut as Troy Flavin uses the ice pick he shot out of the black man's hand to pick buckshot out of Big Baby's buttocks—risking his new white linen suit and delaying his wedding rehearsal.

The terms of Welty's apt title represent the novel's dichotomy of mood—a harshly real cultural environment serving as backdrop for a beautifully imaginative cultural ceremony. In geographical and historical terms the Yazoo-Mississippi Delta was the final Southern frontier, the last stand of the plantation dream. As railroads snaked into the big woods during Reconstruction to clearcut the trees for the lumber mills and to strip the bottoms for the cotton plantations, this historical reiteration of antebellum flush times exploited Southern hopes and fears, drawing ambitious whites and restless blacks into a most ambivalent environment. Sometimes called "the most Southern place on earth," the Delta has been seen more recently as the staging ground for the Great Migration to the North; James C. Cobb's study, which uses the tag phrase for a subtitle, is especially informative on the role of the railroads in the rise and fall of the Delta, as well as the relation of trains and the blues. Cobb's study also confirms many other aspects of the novel, which he does include and praise in his reading of Delta texts; he makes many other interesting, intertextual literary references, especially to the Percy and Fa(u)lkner families (335).

Thus the railroads that had created the Delta in a few decades unmade it just as quickly by drawing off its most important natural and human resources, and Welty's setting in "uneventful" 1923 marked the actual turning point of regional expansion and contraction. So the Fairchild wedding at Shellmound plantation becomes an important event, not just in the Delta's imagined social history but in the cultural constructions of the modern South informing Eudora Welty's first, best novel, *Delta Wedding*—a novel that prefigures many by younger women writers in the post-Southern period, which I will later consider in chapter 10.

Chapter Seven

Ralph Ellison's Railroad Passages

Before *Invisible Man* and After

I was on the verge of change—oh how odd of God to
choose—yet playing Cotch or Georgia Skin or Tonk every
night I wasn't gigging or playing dances in that hall
overlooking the railroad tracks, blowing out my strength
and passion against those east- and west-bound trains.

Ralph Ellison, *Juneteenth*

1

Although most of his career and canon reflect his life outside the
South, Ralph Ellison can be considered a contemporary Southern writer in terms of both his personal origins and his professional concerns. Born Ralph Waldo Ellison in 1914, his ambitious
parents had emigrated west only recently from the deep South to
Oklahoma City, searching for a better life. Like many other Southern black immigrants in the West, they were frustrated in their
quest, as we have seen in the work of William Faulkner and Toni
Morrison. Oklahoma was a historic hotbed of segregation and
night riding; the most destructive race riot of the racially conflicted period following the First World War destroyed the pros-
perous Greenwood section of Tulsa in 1921 (*Juneteenth* 47). The
young Ellison attended college during the darkest years of the
Depression at the famous Tuskegee Institute in Alabama, founded
by the black accomodationist leader Booker T. Washington, who
preached agrarian themes to African Americans, advising them
to find their salvation on the Southern landscape.

Ellison's subsequent career and most of his writing were focused in the North, specifically in New York City and Harlem, but the writer saw himself and his literary personae as products of Southern black life. For Ellison, modern African American culture was created by the Great Migration from South to North, and by delineating his own experience he believed he was forging the consciousness of his race (Lester 123). An important narrative and thematic thrust that may be traced throughout Ralph Ellison's oeuvre involves the difficult journey toward self-awareness, and the motif most often representing it is the historical movement of African Americans in a modern "middle passage" from South to North, from past to future, and from rural roads to city streets—especially as represented by the railroads that facilitated their transitions, for better or worse. Therefore, Ellison and his classic novel, *Invisible Man,* are best understood in terms of contemporary Southern writing within the African American tradition. His career and canon extend the Southern Renaissance as well as the Harlem Renaissance; Ellison shares subject matter and meanings with Southern black writers such as Langston Hughes, Zora Neale Hurston, and Richard Wright, but he also shares ideas and themes with white Southern writers like William Faulkner, Thomas Wolfe, and Robert Penn Warren.

Despite the fact that he published only a single novel during his own lifetime, Ralph Ellison remains one of the most important writers in the African American tradition after the Harlem Renaissance, comparable with Richard Wright and James Baldwin in his generation. A discussion of Ellison's achievement must be centered on *Invisible Man,* but it should not neglect his other writing. Although his single masterpiece seemed to appear from nowhere in 1952, it had a lengthy foreground in Ellison's earlier life and work; likewise, the delay of the long-promised second novel did not negate the considerable body of fiction and nonfiction that Ellison completed after *Invisible Man,* which has been published in various formats. His single novel is a prodigious effort as well, considering virtually all of African American culture within the contexts of the American and Southern majority cultures by combining the epic sweep of traditional narrative with the precise imagery of contemporary poetry.

Invisible Man conflates the history of African Americans with

Ralph Ellison's personal story in ways that recall both sides of the double conciousness posited by W.E.B. Du Bois. Biography and autobiography have been the archetypal forms for the matter of African American life from slave narratives, which developed into autobiographies like Fredrick Douglass's, to contemporary black novels like Toni Morrison's. The romantic idealism and individualism of classic white American literature also influenced Ellison—from the works of his namesake, Ralph Waldo Emerson, and his protégés Henry David Thoreau and Walt Whitman, to the darker visions of Herman Melville, Nathaniel Hawthorne, and Edgar Allan Poe—all of whom appear in various guises in the author's work, along with more contemporary Southern writers like William Faulkner, Thomas Wolfe, and Robert Penn Warren. Perhaps the single most important literary intertext for *Invisible Man* is a book published just a century earlier, Melville's classic *Moby Dick* (1851), one of the first of our fictions to face the dislocations of American culture caused by the industrial revolution in the early nineteenth century. Like Melville's American classic, Ellison's book is a variation of the Bildungsroman, in which the protagonist engages in a quest for maturity and fulfillment leading through a series of difficult personal passages, narratives and themes also discovered in works by Faulkner, Wolfe, and Warren, as we have seen in earlier chapters.

Ellison's novel creates some of these events and themes from his own life and from his earlier writing. His nameless protagonist grows up in the black quarter of a Southern town, attends a patriarchal black college somewhere in the deep South, emigrates to job opportunities in New York City, lives in Harlem where he participates in a wide range of cultural upheavals, and withdraws into his personal world when he realizes his invisibility within white America. As in Melville's classic, as well as in many black and/or Southern narratives both auto/biographical and fictional, Ellison's persona tells his own tale from the perspective of his hard-won insight; in a sense, he realizes his own story and writes his own history. The author's major technical device in this regard becomes the framing envelope; the narrator's hibernation in a nineteenth century sub-cellar beneath the streets of Harlem allows Ellison to project his themes in a surrealistic mode that counterpoints the essential realism of the central narrative structure.

2

In another regard, Ellison works through not only his own life experiences but his earlier artistic efforts as well. Although he was always fascinated by literature, the younger Ellison trained as a musician at Tuskegee and studied sculpture in New York City before he began to write under the influence of social realism in the 1930s and 1940s. His most important model was Richard Wright, and Ellison's early prose echoed Wright's efforts in both fiction and nonfiction. Like the works of his mentor, Ellison's first stories depicted young blacks emigrating from a South symbolic of the traditional agrarian past and immigrating to a North that imaged an uneasy technological future. Often the dramatized events involve the actual transition, the journey itself in the short stories, along with the action before and/or after in longer fictions. For example, several of Ralph Ellison's earliest stories, published only after his death, present an autobiographical protagonist riding freight trains out of the South in the mode of Depression-era social realism that he later transforms in *Invisible Man*.

These stories, as well as Ellison's nonfiction, indicate the author's familiarity with and interest in railroads. Still the most important mode of long-distance travel in his youth and young manhood, trains were also the major means of the Great Migration, as African Americans for the most part were economically unable to purchase automobiles reliable enough for these long journeys. Such was certainly the case with Ellison's family, as they traveled to visit their relatives in the Deep South by circuitous railroad trips during his youth. As a young man in the Depression decade, Ellison became a nonpaying passenger on the freight trains; even leaving for college at Tuskegee, he "grabbed an armful of freight car" in order to save his meager funds (*Territory* 324). This expedient proved something of a lark to the adventurous young writer, until he was forced off the freight train by railroad detectives in Decatur, Alabama, the very town in which the famous case of the Scottsboro boys was then being tried. In the eyes of a young African American, "the trial was a macabre circus, a kangaroo proceeding . . . the ultimate form of racial victimage" (*Territory* 325). Although Ellison managed to elude the detectives in this instance, when he later left Tuskegee for New York City his own trip was by passenger train.

As Ellison began to write, his earlier experiences on "the iron road," as the hobos called it, provided dramatic material for fiction in the mode of Depression-era social realism. His most important examples for this mode were the works of Richard Wright, which themselves were often determined by the movements of freight trains as modes for escape. Like Wright, Ellison often associated railroads with the violent forces of historical determinism, as seen in the Marxist analysis of cultural symbolism then important to both writers. An example in Wright's work is "Big Boy Leaves Home" (1936), while Ellison's "Hymie's Bull" (1937), his first story accepted for publication, proves similar in setting, mode, and theme. (Dates assigned to Ellison's works reflect either the year of first publication or, in the case of the unpublished pieces, the best understanding of the year of composition [*Flying* ix–xxxviii].) Ellison's narrator is a nameless young black man forced to ride the rails in search of work and adventure; many of the personal details seem autobiographical, and the knowledge about boarding "side-door Pullmans" adds an air of realism (*Flying* 85). The central event of the tale is a battle to the death between Hymie, an "ofay," or white transient from Brooklyn and a sadistic railroad "bull," or detective. After Hymie dispatches his antagonist with a switch-blade knife, all the hobo riders are forced to flee rather than reveal the killer. Of course, the Depression-era theme of working-class solidarity among blacks and whites becomes the real point of the story, even if this canard of proletarian realism is rather crudely realized in this apprentice work.

Several other of Ellison's early unpublished stories also feature similar railroad adventures. "I Never Learned Their Names" (1937–38) again recalls Richard Wright's fiction, but this example is more restrained and better crafted. The protagonist is another nameless, autobiographical, young African American riding the rails in search of work in the company of other riders both black and white. As the story opens, the "Santa Fe freight was highballing down a grade in the dark" (*Flying* 89), a metaphorical blackness for the frightened young man clinging to the top of a boxcar in the smoke, cinders, and sparks of a hellish, nightmare version of the

American dream's traditional westward direction. Yet the conflict here is more skillfully resolved than in "Hymie's Bull"; again, the narrator finds solidarity with a white "buddy," Morrie, whom he met in a "sunflower jungle outside an Oklahoma town" (*Flying* 90). In turn, other white people, a displaced elderly couple searching for their son who has been recently released from prison, befriend the protagonist and share their meager provisions. The youngsters are separated from the older couple by the movement of the trains, however, and the story ends with another version of Ellison's autobiographical escape in Decatur, Alabama.

The conflict in "Boy on a Train" (1937–38) proves even more muted, as Ellison seems to recall experiences as a young boy after the early death of his father. Here a widowed African American mother is traveling with her two young sons from Oklahoma City to a new home in McAlester, Oklahoma, shortly after losing her husband. They are riding on the Rock Island line, and Ellison's observations are both precise and suggestive: "A freight was passing . . . so swiftly that its orange-and-red cars seemed a streak of watercolor with gray spaces punched through" (*Flying* 14). The conflict is more subtle here, with a white railway "butcher" or vendor, who sexually harasses the mother, as the antagonist, rather than a railroad policeman who physically threatens the freight car riders. The boy on this train can feel the same sense of injustice in the vendor's attitudes that the detectives in Decatur engendered in Ellison himself and in his first autobiographical narrators; these various uniformed minions of the railroad project its importance as a symbol of a biased cultural determinism that discriminates in terms of race, class, and gender.

One of Ellison's early published stories, "King of the Bingo Game" (1944), uses railroads in a more surrealistic manner, thus underlining this determining symbolism from the earlier pieces and prefiguring *Invisible Man* in terms of literary form. The protagonist is an unemployed African American, a recent arrival in Harlem from the South, desperate to win the cash prize of the bingo game in order to pay for his wife's medical treatment. For several successive nights he has attended the downtown theater where the bingo game is played between the two halves of a movie double bill. As he nods off during the first film, a train whistle on the soundtrack turns his dreams to his home in Rocky Mount,

North Carolina, a major railroad division point on the Atlantic Coast Line. He dreams of racing a train across a trestle, only to have his narrow escape negated by "looking back and seeing with terror that the train had left the track and was following him right down the middle of the street, and all the white people laughing as he ran screaming" (*Flying* 125). However, this surrealistic nightmare of the locomotive's driving wheels is soon supplanted by another involving a dangerous machine; though he scores a "bingo" on one of his cards, he must successfully spin the bingo game's wheel of fortune to win the cash.

At some level, Ellison's persona knows that the game is as much an illusion as the movie that preceded it, a predetermined dream controlled by the white moguls of American popular culture. When he has his chance with the electrically controlled wheel of fortune, he refuses to give up his power as "king of the bingo game." As the unruly crowd screams for him to finish the game, he imagines his situation in terms of a railroad track, here the Harlem subway system's "A" train, which he flees as unsuccessfully as the earlier Southern flyer "because to stop would bring the train crushing down on top of him and to attempt to leave across the other track would mean to run into a hot third rail as high as his waist which threw blue sparks that blinded his eyes until he could hardly see" (*Flying* 134).

The "A Train" is as much an element in popular culture as the "Chattanooga Choo-Choo" or any other mainline flyer, thanks to hits like the Duke Ellington/Billy Strayhorn classic "Take the A Train" (1941, 1957), which became the theme song of the Duke Ellington Orchestra by projecting a dreamy, hip, bi-racial identity for Harlem. The subway proves a very ambiguous symbol within modern American culture, as indicated in chapter 1 above in consideration of works by Allen Tate, William Faulkner, Thomas Wolfe, and others. When the white emcee promises to give the protagonist the prize, he persuades the protagonist to relinquish his control of the bingo game; as soon as the curtain drops, however, two white cops club him into insensibility, a violent conclusion prefiguring that of *Invisible Man,* begun in 1945, a year after "King of the Bingo Game." The novel's use of the railroad and technological images would be much closer to dreamlike surrealism than to social realism.

Another wartime effort, "Flying Home" (1944), also prefigures *Invisible Man* in its musical patterns, as its title derives from Lionel Hampton's 1940 hit of the same title. This story uses the symbolism of an airplane as a machine both transcending beyond and limited by the complexities of American racial history. Undoubtedly suggested by the famous Tuskegee Airmen, the first African American combat flyers in World War II who were trained at Ellison's alma mater, the story also proceeds in a surrealistic mode. "Flying Home" also relates to Ellison's unfinished novel about an African American prisoner of war in Germany, possibly derived from the life experience of black merchant seamen held as prisoners of war under segregated conditions at the request of the Allied Forces.

3

Thus even in his earliest fictions, Ralph Ellison is quickly moving beyond his first mentors and models toward an artistic complexity based on the rhythmic counterpoint of music, the balanced forms of sculpture, and the psychological symbolism of modernist literature. Ellison's first fictions likewise project the meanings as well as the modes of his later works, since the major theme of *Invisible Man* becomes the protagonist's engagement with the destructive, nightmarish machinery of contemporary American life. Although such technology extended into the South—in the form of the railroad, for instance—it pervaded the urban life of the North, where speeding subway trains and rocketing elevator cars provide the most common symbolism in Ellison's long narrative. Unlike his mentor, Richard Wright in *Native Son* (1940), historical machinery in Ellison's novel does not militate for a mechanistic view of history. Ellison develops the actual mechanical images and technological symbols in his novel, but he shows his protagonist resisting them to preserve his human identity and dignity by using technology to his own creative purposes. For example, he steals his electricity from "Monopolated Power" in order to brighten the nineteenth-century sub-cellar where he has hibernated, and to power his phonograph to play his collection of black blues recordings.

Like the blues, which often uses trains for both image and

rhythm, this deterministic vision of the railroad exists within Ellison's novel in both the South and the North. As we might expect, railroads are used as realistic details in both settings, but several instances become more pointedly symbolic. In the Southern sections, roughly the first third of the book, the most important example is found in the funeral train that bears the body of the "Founder" back to the narrator's small black college; this image is evoked by the blind orator, the Reverend Barbee, in a chapel sermon memorializing the fallen leader and affirming the current president, Dr. Bledsoe. Of course, the unnamed founder is based on the historical figure of Booker T. Washington, and Barbee's outline of the founder's career proves quite close to that of Tuskegee's first president.

Like Washington, the "Founder" grew up in slavery, participated in the activities of the Underground Railroad, struggled to find accommodation with the white power structure during Reconstruction and in the era of the New South, and died on a journey to the North raising funds to support his institution. The return of Washington's body to Alabama was like the funeral journey of President Lincoln a generation earlier, and Barbee's sermon recalls the imagery of Walt Whitman's famous elegy for Lincoln, "When Lilacs Last in the Dooryard Bloomed" (1865). Of course, the reversal of directions here, from the Underground Railroad to the funeral train, sets up the narrator's escape to the North from the paternalistic power structure of the South, both white and black, and his frustration to find the same structures firmly in place beyond the Mason-Dixon line. For the accommodationist Barbee, like the historical Booker T. Washington, remains an ambivalent figure, like his statue on the campus that can be interpreted as either unmasking or blindfolding a kneeling slave.

Immediately upon his arrival in New York City, Ellison's protagonist is thrown into the rush of the subway, still headed north to Harlem. He is crammed into the subway car "by the milling pepper-and-salt mob" and crushed against a white woman in such close proximity that he fears the race riot he knows this unintentional liberty would have caused back in the South (*Invisible Man* 140). "The train seemed to plunge downhill now, only to lunge to a stop that shot me out upon a platform feeling like something regurgitated from the belly of a frantic whale" (141).

He has survived his Jonah-like passage into the belly of the beast, in the very bowels of the city, but the next day he repeats his initiatory experience in the vertical rush of a skyscraper's crowded elevator rising above the city. "It rose like a rocket, creating a sensation in my crotch as though an important part of myself had been left below in the lobby" (147). From figurative emasculation in this citadel of the Emerson company's corporate power, Ellison's protagonist will go forth to face the fearful urban machinery of his future.

Even more expressionistic machine images are discovered as Ellison's narrator tries to make his way in the mechanical labyrinth of the metropolis. In particular, the industrial explosion in the Liberty Paints plant where he finds work (a surrealistic vision of contemporary American art) and his subsequent trauma by electric shock therapy in the psychiatric hospital (an ironic symbol of contemporary social institutions) create an image of modern American culture as a self-determined machine, producing the apocalyptic racial discords that precipitate the narrator's final retreat into his sub-cellar. Yet for all of the protagonist's bitter dilemma in the book's concluding frame, *Invisible Man* is not marked by modernist despair. The protagonist's hibernation becomes a sort of religious retreat after he learns something of the white other, promising reengagement when he does emerge to claim his place in the twentieth century by truly understanding his personal and his racial past—much like the vision discovered not just in contemporary black writers but in many white ones as well.

4

In this way, the novel's conclusion prefigures Ellison's later work, which tries to realize a glimpse of American promises and possibilities. His major project was another novel, one that projected a protagonist like the most important of the narrator's many doubles in *Invisible Man*—the trickster figure Rinehart. In the unfinished novel, the protean character morphs and unites a series of takes on contemporary African American culture that appeared as short pieces over the remainder of the author's career. Ellison could never bring the novel to the conclusion he wished, though a text has been assembled from his papers for recent publication by his literary executor and published as *Juneteenth* (2000).

In terms of railroads, the most interesting piece Ellison published himself is the ironically titled "A Song of Innocence" (1970), which appeared in the *Iowa Review* with the note "—Excerpt from a novel in progress" ("Song" 30). The title, recalling William Blake's *Songs of Innocence and Experience,* refers here to the narration by a somewhat autobiographical character, Cliofus, about a boy's life close by the railroad yard in a Southern small town. His odd name suggests the muse of history, Clio, and the construction of history by language is the central theme in this text. Cliofus is subject to physical seizures that propel him back and forth from past to present, seemingly suggesting the dislocations of history itself. As boy and man Cliofus can be soothed only by the visceral rhythms of trains: "When I watch those engines and boxcars and gondolas I start to moving up and down in my body's joy" ("Song" 31). More importantly, he listens to the trains, and their chuffing, whistling, and clanking become a sort of language that takes the place of the ambiguous words that confuse his aching mind. Language creates history in Cliofus's view, and Ellison portrays both with the scatalogical imagery of working-class black men.

The author's questions particularly concern African American history, which emerges as a construct of a hegemonic white American culture. All of these themes and motifs are conflated in the climactic remembrance, when the ironically named white teacher, Miss Kindly, takes Cliofus's "colored school" class on an outing to see a preserved whale mounted in a railroad car, a rather surreal image but one perhaps based on an actual show train touring exhibit between the two world wars (Carstens 30). Ellison seemingly suggests another reading of *Moby Dick* in this sequence, trumping Melville with an image of the American Dream reduced to an absurdist nightmare of a stinking carcass far removed from the sea by the determinations of an industrialized culture. Unlike Melville's Ishmael, Ellison's Cliofus has yet to come to terms with his time or place so as to complete the meaning of his tale.

Juneteenth is certainly the most important of Ralph Ellison's posthumous works, but, as with those of Thomas Wolfe, textual and editorial complications prove problematic for the placement of the text within the overall canon of the Southern Renaissance. Again as with Wolfe, Ellison left thousands of manuscript pages evidently intended as a single massive work, perhaps in an intertextual conversation with William Faulkner (Johnson xxiii). Like Edward Aswell, Ellison's literary executor, John F. Callahan, has selected a strand of this material, combined with a few different pieces to provide perspective, and published the result as a discrete text, the new novel so long anticipated. These textual and editorial processes are too complicated to rehearse here, except to comment that the novel as assembled neglects some materials published earlier by Ellison as a work in progress, such as "A Song of Innocence," and that its reconstructed narrative never quite coheres as a novel. The final product reads more like an anthology or perhaps a short-fiction cycle than a novel, though it presents much brilliant writing. *Juneteenth* also includes several important train sequences that confirm the centrality of railroad imagery and symbolism in Ellison's work.

Although the narrative frame of *Juneteenth* is set in the 1950s, most of its narration is placed in its paired protagonists' streams of consciousness, so that the action ranges from the early years of the century in the Oklahoma Territory to mid-century Washington, D.C. As we have seen earlier, these decades form the Golden Age of American railroading, so the prevalence of tracks and trains in the text exists as realistic detail often used for social purposes, much as in Ellison's earliest stories under the influence of Richard Wright. For example, the black protagonist flees from white mob violence by hiding in an empty boxcar while concealing his murdered brother's infant son, who grows up to become his own "white" cultural antagonist. "Stripped the paper from the boxcar walls to make him a bed then setting there with the car bumping under me wondering why I hadn't let them have him and be free" (*Juneteenth* 313–14).

Their twinned streams of consciousness include many dream sequences, several involving silent movies, which become a major motif. In one the pictured simulacrum of the steam engine threatens to leave the screen and hurtle into the "white sections" and "their favored seats," much as in "The King of the Bingo Game" (234–35). The most important use of railroads is for migration northward, however, though here this symbolic movement is portrayed more complexly as the younger protagonist grows up to become a putatively white U.S. Senator from a Northern state. The novel's most extensive railroad scene combines these several modes of presentation in a surrealistic nightmare of a hellbound journey as the senator lies dying after an assassination attempt by his unacknowledged, multi-racial, surrogate son. "It was a long freight, and far up the tracks he could see the engine, pouring a billowing plume of smoke against the sunny landscape as with a nervous, toy-like shuttling of driving-rods it curved the rails to the west" (322–28).

Just as important as these later fictions are the two volumes of nonfiction, *Shadow and Act* (1964) and *Going to the Territory* (1986), which collect Ellison's thoughtful criticism of African American culture—especially of literature, music, and art. Certainly, Ellison left an extensive body of work, one that would make him a notable African American writer, even without the major achievement of *Invisible Man,* perhaps among the dozen best individual books by black Americans. In many ways, Ellison pioneered the continuing Renaissance of contemporary African American letters represented by major figures like Ernest Gaines and Toni Morrison, a contemporary extension of the Harlem Renaissance. His career and canon are both rooted in the Southern Renaissance, however, showing him as one of our most important contemporary Southern writers in the African American tradition. Among the elements that make Ellison's body of work so memorable are his vision of the quest for African American selfhood within the pull of place and the rush of time, as imaged by the nightmarish machinery of contemporary America—especially by his ambivalent railroad passages.

Chapter Eight

Robert Penn Warren's Postmodern Poetic Railroads

Ballads and Recollections

John Henry said to the Captain, "A man ain't nuthin but a man."

Robert Penn Warren, *Incarnations: Poems 1966–1968*

1

As we discovered in chapter 5, images of tracks and trains observed or traveled pervade Warren's writing in all genres, particularly his prose fiction, just as they crowded his early life in the Golden Age of Southern railroads. Some of these instances, especially in the novels and stories, may be explained as simply realistic observation and reportage of the era in which railroads still remained a dominant force in Southern culture. However, Warren's contextualizing of these images in works of all genres most often suggests his focusing themes of place, time, and self-identity. The present chapter will extend our reading of Warren's railroad imagery to his poetry, both generally considered and in several paired, particular examples. Although Warren was first and last a poet, his breakthrough success with *All the King's Men* in 1946 determined his initial place within the development of the Southern Renaissance as the presumptive heir of William Faulkner's and Thomas Wolfe's fictive heritage. More recent scholarship on the Southern Renaissance and Robert Penn Warren has been forced to acknowledge the preeminence of his poetry within both canons. Indeed, his poems may capture more forcefully many aspects of his matter and meaning, including his real and recreated railroads in his postmodern ballads and recollections.

While considering the poetry, we should not neglect the railroad memories that Warren shared with other writers of the Southern Renaissance like Faulkner and Wolfe. The most important of these remains his boyhood in the busy rail junction of Guthrie, Kentucky, developed above. When the young Warren exhausted the limited educational resources Guthrie offered, he commuted on the local accommodation train to finish high school in nearby Clarksville, Tennessee. His train travels extended to Nashville in 1920, home to both the Dixie Line and Vanderbilt University—recently renamed for its railroad-owning patron. The same railroad network that delivered young Red Warren opened a much larger world to the "Athens of the South," a prospering metropolitan center already home to a burgeoning literary coterie. Although Vanderbilt remained a Methodist backwater in some ways, Warren and his fellow Fugitives read *The Waste Land* in 1922, the year of its initial publication. After reading and memorizing the modernist epic, Robert Penn Warren was committed to poetry for a lifetime (Blotner *Warren* 35–36).

The Collected Poems of Robert Penn Warren (1998), ably edited by John Burt, gathers poems that first appeared between 1922 and the poet's death in 1989. Not all of these hundreds of poetic texts prove exemplary, of course, but these accomplishments earned Warren two Pulitzer Prizes for poetry in 1957 and 1979, the first official Poet Laureateship in 1986, and just about every other poetic honor possible. Probably the most striking qualities of this massive body of work are its consistent quality and its incredible complexity. Warren's poetry develops through several distinct phases: apprenticeship pieces; early modern efforts under the influence of Eliot; poetic epic in *Brother to Dragons: A Tale in Verse and Voices* (1953); the more personal lyrics of *Promises* (1957) and after; the personal epic in *Audubon: A Vision* (1966); and finally the amazing accomplishments of his final two decades, a "poetic renascence" Harold Bloom compares to "the final phases of Thomas Hardy, William Butler Yeats, and Wallace Stevens" (xxiii).

Such critical praise and scholarly difficulty are confirmed

both by careful consideration of Warren's railroad imagery generally and by the close reading of two narrative poems that configure his use of railroad images in particular: "Ballad: Between the Boxcars (1923)" (1960) and "Recollection in Upper Ontario, From Long Before" (1980). Interestingly enough, though separated by two decades in the Warren canon, both project a powerful ambivalence enhanced by intertextual connections with works by two other writers—Cleanth Brooks's critical reading of the former and William Meredith's poetic response to the latter. Although "Ballad: Between the Boxcars (1923)" and "Recollection in Upper Ontario, From Long Before" remain Warren's two most important deployments of the train as trope, railroad imagery may be discovered from his earliest to his latest work in *The Collected Poems*.

Early apprentice works, often influenced by T.S. Eliot, include the ironically titled "The Limited" (1933), which separates wan lovers on the steps of a departing Pullman car and plays with the multiple meanings of the title in the manner of Flannery O'Connor. In the biographically important "The Return: An Elegy" (1934), the protagonist is placed behind the Pullman car's windowpane to contemplate a symbolic landscape while returning home for his mother's funeral, and later lies alone locked in the coffin-like "roaring cubicle" of a Pullman berth (*Poems* 34). Other interesting examples of Warren's earlier poems referencing railroads include "Terror" (1941) and "Original Sin: A Short Story" (1942), both collected in *Eleven Poems on the Same Theme;* in each the suggestion is made that old guilt feelings pursue the poetic personae by the ineluctable path of the rails, "Riding the rods, perhaps—or grandpa's will paid the ticket" (*Poems* 69).

Warren's return to lyric poetry in *Promises* (1957) presents the railroad as a personal, perhaps postmodern, symbol at several levels, from a youthful play train in "What Was the Promise That Smiled from the Maples at Evening" to the battered boxcars of more recent observation in "Walk by Moonlight in Small Town" to the more fantastic "slime on the railroad rails" of "Dragon Country" (*Poems* 132). The first of these two poems is dedicated "To Gabriel," Warren's then infant son, making the shoe-box train of Warren's own youth an appropriate memory to maintain family continuities that would eventuate a decade later in a scale model railroad set, which father and son constructed in the attic of their Connecticut home. Both the poetic and the actual toy trains also recall several images in Warren's fiction: little Jeb's shoe-box train in "Blackberry Winter" and Bolton Lovehart's circus trains in "The Circus in the Attic."

"Tale of Time, IV. The Interim" (1966) presents an important autobiographical reference from Squigtown, the African American section on the "other side of the tracks" in south Guthrie; Warren and his family visit their old, sick, and dying black nurse, probably sometime during the Depression, and the L&N tracks with their westward passing "night freight" again symbolize the inexorable passage of time for all, black and white (*Poems* 189). The poem also proves remarkable for its attempt to come to terms with the other—here old, black, female, and poor, but still part of the poet's own family in several human senses. "The Ballad of Mr. Dutcher and the Last Lynching in Gupton" (1974) also concerns the death of the other, though here demonstrating the darker side of Guthrie's railroad history in the dramatization of an actual lynching in the 1920s.

"Convergences" (1981), structured by an extended image of twinned rails converging in the dark maw of a frightening railroad tunnel and a narrative of encountering a mysterious stranger, provides a good example of railroad images of tramps seen earlier in both fiction ("Blackberry Winter" [1946]) and poetry ("Recollection in Upper Ontario, From Long Before" [1980]), which are extended into Warren's final period. Even *Altitudes and Extensions* (1985), Warren's final volume of poetry, includes a brace of railroad poems, "Whistle of the 3 A.M." and "Last Night Train," which are paired on facing pages to extend the ambivalence of rail images from the poet's early adolescence in Kentucky, concerned only with self, to his advancing age in Connecticut, where again he encounters the other in the guise of another shabby, aging, impoverished black woman in a commuter-train coach— texts to which we will later return.

Also, at least a dozen other railroad references are incorporated in his other works, including one chosen from a traditional railroad ballad, "John Henry," that serves as epigraph for both the seventh poem, "The Self That Stares"—in the sequence "Garland for You" in the collection *You, Emperors and Others* (1960)— and as one of two for the entire volume *Incarnations* (1968) (*Poems*

153, 221). Of course, the ballad's man-versus-machine narrative—where John Henry, a legendary figure originally associated with the actual Chesapeake and Ohio Rail Road, chooses death before defeat by the new steam-powered rock drill—creates some interesting intertextualities, not just for the poems in these particular gatherings but for all of Warren's railroad images.

2

Robert Penn Warren's own railroad "ballad" is actually a sequence comprised of three short poems in different forms, all three concerning diverse aspects of a fifteen-year-old's fatal fall from a freight train at an unnamed Southern rail junction sometime in 1923. The Southern setting and the specific date suggest a possible source in the poet's Kentucky background, though Warren indicated his narrative was generalized, a suggestion that complements the universal themes of this cautionary tale, making a biographical source unnecessary for full understanding. At fifteen, the poem's protagonist balances between youth and manhood, old enough to try a man's role by "grabbing" a freight, but too young to hold on to his place aboard the speeding train. Unlike other youthful exploits and mishaps mentioned in the poem, these events prove unforgiving, as his young life is crushed "between the boxcars." These misadventures recall Ralph Ellison's reminiscences and fictions about riding the rails of the South in the Depression decade.

Section 1, "I Can't Even Remember the Name," presents this fateful event in the form, though not in the exact style nor the tone, of a traditional ballad. The poet uses five stanzas of four lines each, rhyming *abab;* in fact, the ten first and third lines end in only five rhyming words ("fell . . . yell . . . well . . . tell . . . hell") while the ten second and fourth lines all conclude with the refrain "between the boxcars." However, these attenuated lines of twelve to fourteen syllables in varied feet, as well as the overall "smart aleck" tone, though appropriate to the protagonist, create the feeling of a ballad gone awry in the postmodernist mode Warren often favors in later work. In particular, these variations on ballad form shift the interest from the subject, as in traditional railroad ballads like "John Henry," "Casey Jones," or "Hobo Bill," to the narrator. As the last stanza puts its theme,

Suppose I remembered his name, then what the hell
Good would it do him now between the boxcars?
But it might mean something to me if I could tell
You the name of the one that fell between the boxcars.
(*Poems* 165)

The second-person pronoun of the last line also engages the reader in teasing out the meaning of this terrible occurrence, a practice Warren favors with first-person narrators in fiction and philosophical personae in poetry; his several variations on the ballad provide good examples—especially "The Ballad of Billie Potts" (1944) and "Ballad of a Sweet Dream of Peace" (1957).

In section 2, "He Was Formidable," emphasis shifts back to the lost boy as the narrator describes his protagonist's youthful prowess both on the local baseball team and with the town's teenage girls. Beyond this narrative data, the speaker projects a future for the fifteen-year-old in the big leagues of both professional baseball and amateur romance, all recorded in tabloid headlines—as he would have been "formidable" indeed. Other imagined futures follow as a supermarket manager, a research scientist, and a military leader—all bringing the narrative closer to the present of 1960 than the past of 1923. The long, formless verse paragraphs of this section are typical of Warren's middle period, and they share only the refrain, "between the boxcars," with the opening section. Here the phrasing grows ever more harsh and nightmarish—finally climaxing in the final verse paragraph:

. . . when that blunt grossness, slam-banging, bang-
  slamming,
                          blots black
                          the last blue flash of sky. (*Poems* 166)

These "blunt," repetitive rhythms recreate the mechanical progress of technology as represented by the intrusion of the "formidable" freight train into the delicate beauties of the American dream of nature.

"Ballad Between the Boxcars (1923)" is only one of several "story" poems Cleanth Brooks considers in an article on Warren's narrative poems. All of Brooks's readings are insightful, as we would expect from this cogent critic who was also Warren's life-long friend and a collaborator on such New Critical texts as *Understanding Poetry* (1938). As Brooks observes, the train moves through American space and time like the force of time/history: "How heedless it sometimes seems; how ruthless as it speeds along; how rapidly it moves into the future" (Brooks 136). When the individual impinges on its unswerving path he may be carried or crushed, just as nature impersonally disposes of human agency to its own ends, even though its actions may prove beneficent or detrimental to the individual. Brooks points out the efficacy of Warren's textual image: "The newspaper whirled down the track when the through freight has passed" (*Poems* 166). However, most important in Brooks's view is that even in the midst of danger and destruction we should realize our human brotherhood; it might be possible that "We may know the poor self not alone, but with all who are cast / To that clobber and slobber and grunt, between the boxcars" (*Poems* 48). Brooks also connects the text with other anecdotal poems that establish identity through consciousness of darker and brighter possibilities in the self and in others: see, for example, "Dragon Country" (1957), mentioned above as a source of a fantastic railroad image, "Old Nigger on One-Mule Cart Encountered Late at Night When Driving Home from Party in Back Country" (1975), another poem about coming to terms with the racism of the regional past, and "Speleology" (1979), which connects with the novel *The Cave* (1959) by exploring the dark journey all must make into self.

Brooks seems to have considered the version of "Ballad Between the Boxcars" that Warren published in *Selected Poems, 1923–1975* (1976), one that omitted the third section—increasing unity but limiting complexity in the overall text. In any case, Brooks is silent on section 3, "He Has Fled," as the speaker becomes more philosophical about his protagonist's hard fate. Formally, Warren employs anaphora by opening each of nine short verse paragraphs, arranged in three triads, with the third-person pronoun "He"; the final triad varies the openings and shifts the emphasis to "we," further weaving his audience into the narrative and its completed meaning. A thoughtful tone stitches together protagonist and persona, nature and individual, time and space, in the manner of Warren's most successful work of his middle period, *Audubon* (1969). Yet even in this dreamlike transcendence Warren employs railroad imagery:

> He has fled like the glint of glory down April-wet
>   rails, toward sunset . . .
> He has fled like the wild goose . . .
>   to brood where the last, lost spur of
>   The Canadian Pacific ends. (*Poems* 166)

The conclusion of the section and of the ballad turns to the speaker and his puzzlement at this "recollection" that will not leave him (*Poems* 167), one that projects the ambivalence of the railroad as symbol and image of freedom and determinism both in American poetry and in Warren's poems.

3

Another, later poem, "Recollection in Upper Ontario, From Long Before," recreates many of the images and themes discovered in Warren's railroad ballad. First published in 1979, this poetic "recollection" follows the loose form of most poems in the postmodern part of Warren's canon; lines of irregular rhythms and varying lengths are gathered in stanzas of uneven heft. Perhaps this informal structure represents the poet's ambiguous feelings about a recurring nightmare from his youth in a small Southern railroad junction, which haunts him even into his age on a trip to the wilds of the far North. His anxious, confessional tone seems to reveal the genuine ambivalence of personal experience, though in this case we may conclude that the event is fictional. In his later volume of history and reminiscence, *Jefferson Davis Gets His Citizenship Back* (1980), Warren implies that his models for the poem's unfortunate couple were Guthrie denizens, Jeff and Mandy Davis, who died much later and less dramatically in reality than in the recollection (*Davis* 11–14, 108–10).

In the poetic recollection, the couple become Zack and Mag, "pore ole white trash" (*Poems* 386), a drunk and a cripple married out of mutual need and living off the detritus and the charity of the town. In his dream, the speaker is threatened by a speeding locomotive, a "brass-bound eight-wheeler" coming straight toward him (*Poems* 386). However, the dream replays the fate of "Old Zack" and "Old Mag," "out to scrounge coal off the L&N tracks" (*Poems* 386). The brogan Mag wears on her clubfoot is caught "In a switch-V—the coal chute starts here" (*Poems* 387). Zack rushes to her despite the threatening train, but it is unclear to the watching boy if the old man tries to free the old woman's foot or force it deeper into the death grip of the converging rails. "Time stops like it is no-Time" (*Poems* 387). Even the express halts, briefly, and its personnel and passengers pour out to wrap Mag's dismembered corpse in bloody Pullman sheets and report the death to the "news-sheet" as "An accident . . ." (*Poems* 387).

In response to this recurring nightmare from his youth, the aging speaker now recalls two other dreamlike scenes that followed: drunken Zack confronts the boy for suspecting him of Mag's death, protesting his innocence, and the maturing boy imagines the couple's sexual relations or lack thereof. Then the speaker awakens to the dawn's glory in the far North all these years later, to campfires and breakfast, canoes and lakes, "on the unrippling sheen / Of the day's silver and gold" (*Poems* 388). The poem ends with his ambivalent questions; first, is this

> The same world I stood in,
> In the ditch, years ago,
> And saw what I saw?

And finally, even more ambivalently, he wonders,

> Or what did I see? (*Poems* 388)

Certainly, one answer here is the penetration of the archetypal machine, the "brass-bound" locomotive, into the silver and gold dream of nature, if only in the haunted nightmare of the poet-speaker perhaps recreating the archetypal transition of American dream to American nightmare.

Warren dedicated this railroad "recollection" to the contemporary poet Richard Eberhart, a longtime friend, and one interesting response to its puzzling ambivalence is found in a piece by another friend and poet, William Meredith. "Not Both" appears in Meredith's collection *The Cheer* (1980), printed on a single page opposite to a page-long quotation from Warren's poem. This extended epigraph is actually seven lines longer than Meredith's poem, and it contains all of the central nightmare up to the point of Mag's death. Meredith's persona quickly sums up the major question:

> The club-footed woman was mangled by the train.
> Her husband was trying to free her foot from the switch-V
> or he was holding her there so the train would kill her.
> (16)

Meredith's poem then compares three situations involving possible incest, suicide, and betrayal, concluding with two cryptic single-line stanzas:

> Somebody knows or nobody knows these answers.
>
> One of those appalling things is true too. (16)

Applying Meredith's formulations to Warren's narrative forces the reader to contemplate the dark heart of the mystery created by Mag's death. If someone knows the answer, it must be Zack in his guilt for this terrible act; if no one knows the answer, such universal, blind ignorance proves just as appalling. Following this ruthless logic, Warren's persona becomes even more intriguing: either the innocent butterfly collector intuited the "answer" through the psychological imagery of railroads, or the mature speaker has recognized it through his ongoing nightmare of remembered trains penetrating his timeless dream of nature.

4

Although a few other passing trains are found in the poems comprising Warren's final volume, *Altitudes and Extensions* (1989), the paired railroad poems, "Whistle of the 3 A.M." and "Last Night Train," sum up the poet's earlier railroad ballads and recollections. In fact, the first of the two combines both ballad and recollection by way of its ballad-like *abab* stanza form and its matter recollected from youth in the back country. An aging persona, perhaps awakening to the sound of a passing aircraft, remembers the nightly, nocturnal whistling of the 3 A.M. express racing past his flag-stop town. As a boy he had awakened to the sound and the "magisterial" sweep of the headlight and imagined whirling across the country in his own "darkened cubicle," peering disdainfully from the window of his Pullman berth at "some straggle of a town" much like Guthrie (*Poems* 576). Although these images hearken back to Thomas Wolfe and William Faulkner, Warren is quick to move beyond any nostalgia, thinking now of the silence from "thirty-five thousand feet," "the sandblast of History," and the local graveyard where none care that "The schedule's gone dead of the 3 A.M." (*Poems* 577). "Last Night Train" employs a more open, contemporary poetic form to confront its decidedly post-Southern subject matter. Here, the aging, alienated speaker rides the last commuter train of the night from New York City to the Connecticut suburbs, but his diction recalls earlier recollections in poems like "Ballad Between the Boxcars":

> In that slick and new-fangled coach we go slam-banging
> On rackety ruin of a roadbed, past caterpillar—
> Green of last light on deserted platform. (*Poems* 577)

Most interesting here is the realistic detail of the dilapidated railroad bed of the Northeast Corridor used to symbolize the determination of the late twentieth century by the early nineteenth.

The car is almost deserted, only the narrator and another, sleeping passenger remain—"black, female, middle-aged" but regal and vibrant in "A purple dress. Straps of white sandals" (*Poems* 577). She slumbers on as he alights at his station, guiltily wondering if he should awaken her; then the sound of a "last cricket" makes him nostalgic for "A country lane, late night, late autumn—and there / Alone, again I stand, part of all" (*Poems* 577). In the sky, "The complex of stars is steady in its operation," while the smell of "salt sedge" drifting from Long Island Sound makes him "think of swimming, naked and seaward" (*Poems* 577). Looking up the tracks at the train receding into the night toward Bridgeport, the persona feels like "blessing" the sleeping person who has led him around to seeing things aright even amidst all the roar of contemporary urban life (*Poems* 578).

If Warren's poems prove intertextual with contemporary

poets outside the South such as Richard Eberhart and William Meredith, they become even more so in terms of contemporary Southern poets such as James Dickey and Dave Smith. Even more than in the traditions of Southern fiction, the poetic legacy of the Fugitive/Agrarians persists toward the postmodern, albeit altered over time by variations in matter, transmutations of form, and transformations of theme and meaning. In fact, the very best of contemporary Southern poetry exists in creative tensions of place and time with the earlier father figures like Warren. Chapter 9 will focus on the poetic intertextuality between the railroad images of Robert Penn Warren and Dave Smith, especially in terms of the younger poet's dialogic "roundhouse voices" as they counterpoint the languages of labor and literature within the traditions of the Southern Renaissance.

Chapter Nine

Dave Smith's Post-Southern Railroad Poetry

The Roundhouse Voices

I start here with a tale of the South
. . . .
I could see the moon-faces inside, just boys
like me, fire-haulers, gandies for trains,
white plates steaming
with beans, meat, and fresh bread.

I thought: I will eat meat on that china.
My head was drunk with the possibility.

Dave Smith, "The History of the Queen City Hotel"

1

Although many parts of his career and canon reflect his life outside the South, Dave Smith is very clearly identified as a contemporary Southern poet, both by himself and by other poets and
critics. Certainly his personal background in eastern Virginia and
western Maryland seem Southern enough, as does his present
professional situation at Louisiana State University, where he
figuratively fills the chair of Robert Penn Warren as poetry editor of the *Southern Review*. Between these parts of his life, Smith
has lived in and written about several places outside the South,
ranging from the American West to western Europe, but he has
always returned to variations of his Southern identity in personal, professional, and poetic terms. In his persistent explora-

tion of both the Southern cultural heritage and the contemporary poetic situation, Smith recalls his most important literary progenitors, Warren in particular. In fact, Smith's recent poetry reconsiders the major conflicts and contradictions of Southern culture in confronting the elusive other of race, gender, and, especially, class through innovations of genre, mode, and form—including the use of railroads as image and symbol. For these reasons, Dave Smith is one of our most interesting and important contemporary Southern poets, particularly as his work extends the post-Southern heritage of the Southern Renaissance.

The carefully maintained dichotomy of Dave Smith's two Southern settings, the Chesapeake estuaries and the Allegheny mountains, indicates the poet's concern with place and time, with seascape and landscape, with picture and narrative. For example, photography often serves as a major symbolic motif, so that his narratives frequently shape the continuities of frozen moments caught in photographs. As we discovered in Eudora Welty's fiction, photography inherently juxtaposes nature and technology in matter and in form. Fishing craft predominate in Smith's coastal pictures, railroads in his mountain landscapes, while his human narratives explore the harsh lives of hardworking fishermen and railroaders. Although Hampton Roads is the terminus for major railroads hauling coal to the Tidewater, they almost never appear in Smith's recreated littoral.

In his Appalachians, however, he considers the important east/west coal carriers—in particular, the employers of his grandfather and his uncles at the significant railroad junction of Cumberland, Maryland. His important poems on this family connection include "Cumberland Station" (1977) and "The Roundhouse Voices" (1985), while his wife's family provides materials for "Toy Trains in the Landlord's House" (1983) and "Southern Crescent" (1992). Dave Smith's railroad voices also advance pervasive themes perhaps influenced by Robert Penn Warren: the inertia of place, the weight of time, and the frightful fragility of the self in the face of these forces.

Born and raised in the coastal low country around Portsmouth, Virginia, Dave Smith's first important collection of poetry, *The Fisherman's Whore* (1974), tried to strike a balance between the harsh beauty of the coastal waterways and the hard lives of the Chesapeake water men. For example, his title poem represents both the major matter and the typical form of his early work: tough, terse diction and packed yet concise lines working within orderly, if dense, stanzas and long, often periodic sentences. Some poetic forebears extend back through other American contemporaries like Theodore Roethke and James Wright, to earlier figures as different as Edgar Allan Poe and Walt Whitman, and as far back as the traditional Anglo-Saxon bards of "The Seafarer" and "The Wanderer." Although insistent in staking out his poetic place and his place in contemporary poetry, the collection certainly marked Dave Smith as a young poet worth watching for further developments.

Cumberland Station (1976) presents the other part of the poet's Southern roots in the Allegheny mountain country around Cumberland, Maryland. Here the young writer enjoyed long visits with working-class grandparents, uncles, and cousins representing other masculine traditions of nature and sport, as well as working and wandering—especially in terms of railroads. With this new matter Smith's poetic form evolved in different directions, in particular toward more extended personal narratives in looser verse structures. Again, the title piece proves a good example by using the now abandoned depot of Cumberland as the symbolic nexus of the railroad, representing not just regional history but national developments and personal progress as well.

The maturing persona returns to an important scene of his youth, the small city's deserted railroad depot. Once the heart of a thriving railroad town, Cumberland's station is now a mute monument to America's post-industrial decline and to the poet's loss of personal attachments in this place. Diction and rhythm are still taut but open to more variation and diversification of lines, sentences, and stanzas. The central narrative thrust of the poet's return is hedged with sidebars of other lives, alternative experiences, and different meanings. Literary influences include not just the examples mentioned above but also James Dickey, Lewis Simpson, James Wright, Robert Lowell, Richard Hugo, and other contemporary American writers trying to make sense of the 1970s.

All of Dave Smith's dichotomies of theme unfold in "Cumberland Station": nature and culture, past and present, and picture and narrative. The decaying depot, the symbolic temple of the nineteenth century's new technological dispensation, once dominated the region with its

> Gray brick, ash, hand-bent railings, steps so big
> it takes hours to mount them, polished oak
> pews holding the slim hafts of sun . . . (*Wick* 188)

Now it has become a deserted relic of the twentieth century in a rust-belt waste land, fouled by the detritus of industrial technology—"ash," "soot," and "dirt"—so that even the river is "sored," even its fish soiled (*Wick* 188–89). And this degeneration of the environment is matched by the declension of the speaker's family fortunes. The grandfather, once the ticket master of the station, lives on "in jobless, friendless Cumberland" (*Wick* 189), deserted in death by his friend, Big Daddy, the steam engineer. A son, the speaker's "roundhouse" uncle, is also dead, as is that uncle's son, his hard-drinking cousin. A set of images telescopes those of environmental, cultural, and personal failures:

> In this vaulted hall
> I think of all the dirt poured down
> From shovels and trains and empty pockets.

The living left in Cumberland are as disposable as yesterday's *Pittsburgh Post-Gazette* left on one of the benches in the waiting room and now "snatched up" by a stranger "with the look of a demented cousin" (*Wick* 189).

Back for the latest funeral, the speaker also deserts his grandfather, internalizes the rootless poverty about him, and contemplates some framed photographs of railroad subjects in the empty station. These bits of "bad news" are all he can discover on his trip "home," in contrast to the happier days represented by the photographs of cheering crowds and steam locomotives in the halcyon days of Cumberland's station, when he came here filled with hope of leaving for a larger world.

> Six rows of track, photographed, gleam, rippling
> Like water on walls where famous engineers steam . . .

old news, photographs
Of dead diesels behind chipped glass. (*Wick* 188–89)

In a final gesture of remembrance, piety, and rebellion, the speaker steals a framed photograph of the scrapped locomotives as a memento mori (*Wick* 189).

Cumberland, Maryland, was an important junction of the Baltimore and Ohio and the Western Maryland railroads, major east/west coal carriers; both companies maintained major rail service facilities at Cumberland that employed a large number of local residents in blue collar jobs. The economic changes that struck the region and the railroad industry in the period following the Second World War had a profound effect on Cumberland. Like many rust-belt cities, however, Cumberland has restored its fortunes to some extent, in the process restoring its downtown and refurbishing its railroad station, complete with a steam-powered scenic railroad as a tourist attraction, a sort of full-scale, post-Southern, model-railroad version of the real Western Maryland.

2

Dave Smith's drive toward variety and diversity continued in his next collection, *Goshawk, Antelope* (1979), a book shaped to a great extent by his Western experience of living in Salt Lake City while teaching at the University of Utah. His response to a new environment, just as beautiful and demanding as his earlier sea and landscapes, drew him toward more abstraction and expressionism. The title poem provides a pattern for the whole volume by juxtaposing two totemic creatures within the context of the West and with the poet's earlier development. Deeper echoes of past encounters with animal vitality and human nature appear as recollections of archetypal family experiences, including avatars of father and mother figures, realized in dreamlike narratives marked by precision of diction and syntax, of structure and sound.

Such modes are developed in Smith's two succeeding collections, *Dream Flights* (1981) and *Homage to Edgar Allan Poe* (1981), which extend themselves toward narratives like nightmares discovered both in the human psyche and in the alienation of contemporary America. The best of the 1981 dream sequences include"Homage to Edgar Allan Poe," "Artificial Niggers," with its allusion to Flannery O'Connor's story having a similar title, and "The Pornography Box," a provocative fantasia on a dead father's memorial collection of pornographic pictures. The long title piece of the extended literary homage also proves particularly effective; in six discrete sections its central narrative conflates Poe's literal and literary personae with Smith's own, perhaps in recognition of the dark side of all literary creativity. Smith's style moves alternately toward tighter, more traditional forms in the manner of Poe and toward looser, more diverse forms in the post-Southern mode. Certainly one of the most fascinating aspects of Dave Smith's career is his astonishing virtuosity with verse forms.

New balances and accommodations are discerned in succeeding volumes, *In the House of the Judge* (1983) and *The Roundhouse Voices* (1985), especially as the latter is also a selected poems demonstrating Smith's development through the earlier volumes. The new poems in both books present a mature control of disparate elements, at once more abstracted and more real, more accepting and more confrontational, as well as more formal and more relaxed. After an introductory section developing the symbolism of houses, the three parts of the 1983 volume consider his youth in his two sections of the South and his maturity in a rented house in northern Pennsylvania. In the title poem and in others like "Toy Trains in the Landlord's House," the speaker realizes how we must accept the worlds that others have built for themselves and for us, even as we inherit them and are in many senses determined by them.

"The Roundhouse Voices" serves as an introduction for the 1985 selection, extending the metaphor of houses and homes, in this case with a dialogue of ancestral voices prophesying the inevitable movement of time that defines how we emerge from the past of others into our own identity. Smith did well to choose this long effort as the title piece of his first selected poems, as it represents the several poetic narratives, themes, and styles—or dialogic voices—which had emerged as artistic possibilities during his maturation as a poet.

In point of fact, the real subject of the poem becomes the

speaker's post-Southern transformation of the working-class voices he grew up with into the poetry-class voices of his own maturity. The imagery and symbolism of railroads also proves appropriate, as some of Smith's best poetry centers on subject matter—canals and tracks, trains and boats—that probes the ambivalence of technology, especially in the abandoned station at Cumberland.

In the fugal dialogue that gives the poem its title and structure, "The Roundhouse Voices" extends the major dichotomies discovered earlier in "Cumberland Station." These two very personal railroad poems pair neatly in terms of the two railroad structures contrasted in their titles, imagery, and symbols. The station was the public face of the railroad, while the roundhouse was the mechanical heart of the system, where the massive mountain locomotives, both steam and diesel, were once serviced and prepared for their provision of power to the overall rail network. Like the station, the roundhouse is now closed, decaying and deserted; the speaker, returning for his uncle's funeral, revisits the roundhouse and remembers its dialogic voices from the past—in particular those of the dead uncle, a roundhouse mechanic, and the rail-yard guard, now long dead also. It is possible that both the uncle and the constantly "wheezing" roundhouse guard might have died of silicosis, an industrial disease often affecting railroad workers, as intimated in an earlier scene: "the soot cut into our lungs with tiny diamonds" (*Wick* 85).

In terms of cultural constructions, the roundhouse and rail yard, where the speaker sneaks in to practice baseball, are juxtaposed to the big-league ballparks, other dream places of the adolescent speaker, who saw himself emerging as the next "Mick" Mantle under the tutelage of his uncle. The roundhouse uncle, frustrated at his fate as another bit of industrial waste, presents one hard voice urging his nephew to find a better craft and life; the other, harsher voice is provided by the wheezing railroad guard, with his ironic refrain, *"Who the goddamn hell are you, kid?"* (*Wick* 86, italics in original). The adolescent easily escaped these figures of an interrogating authority, but after the loss of his uncle and the guard, now into his own middle years, he feels the rush of time and the weight of place threatening to destabilize the precarious identity he has established in the dream of

literary success after the failure of his youthful dreams of baseball stardom.

> All day I have held your hand, trying to say back that life,
> To get under that fence with words I lined
> And linked up and steamed into a cold room
> Where the illusion of hope means skin torn in boxes
> Of tools. (*Wick* 87)

The poem's diction, in particular the constant repetition of "voices"
and "words," suggests that at least one of its subjects is the poet/
persona's relation to his literary as well as laboring forbears. Just
as his uncle could not coach him into the working world of the
railroad, much less the big leagues of baseball, the breathless
railroad cop, worn out in several senses, has caught up to ask
him in the poem's final line: "*Who the hell are you, kid?*" (*Wick* 87,
emphasis in original).

3

In the later volumes, Smith's railroad memories pair with his
wife's family background to project themes of time, history, and
identity in poems such as "Toy Trains in the Landlord's House"
and "Southern Crescent." The speaker's father-in-law, a widowed
judge, solaces himself with toy trains and alcohol in the superannuated mansion of a Pennsylvania hill town reminiscent of
Cumberland. Staying in the judge's "white, austere, winterlong
drafty / son of a bitch" of a home (*House* 78), Smith's persona
discovers the old man's toy train set-up in the basement. Decaying like the house and town around it, the model railroad layout
still has some spark of life, which the narrator discovers when he
throws the main switch with a sense of discovery. Interestingly
enough, model trains are often used in literary works as symbols
of artistic endeavor, often misplaced; writers of the Southern Renaissance including William Faulkner, Thomas Wolfe, Eudora
Welty, and Robert Penn Warren provide interesting examples, as
we have seen in several earlier chapters.

On a small scale, the model railroad reiterates the American
dream gone to nightmare in the great wreck of the house, like a

structure in Poe, and the dying town recalling Cumberland. In a final attempt to retain his dream vision, the judge recreates his town in miniature, but now even this last gasp after order is dying away, much like Bolton Lovehart's in Warren's "The Circus in the Attic." Although the speaker realizes the futility of the judge's gesture, he also recognizes that this creative craft mirrors his own, especially in the judge's attempt to proclaim himself "*innocent, innocent, innocent*" of the time, place, and change that trains, even toy or model trains, may represent (*House* 79, emphasis in original). As the speaker maintains the mildewed models, like the dilapidated home, in the absence of the patriarchal judge, he learns about his own personal and professional identity as well.

The toys make an interesting connection with the judge's Christmastime death recorded in "Southern Crescent" (1992), which recounts the couple's return to the South by train after the funeral. Smith takes his epigraph from an early railroad brochure that describes the inaugural "Crescent Limited" in 1891. "*The Crescent Limited . . . will . . . cross the wide stream of the stately Potomac, pass the historic spot where the best blood of the country was poured in its great civil strife. . . .*" (193, ellipses and italics in original). A century later, the ghost of this nineteenth-century promise becomes a prefiguration of a twentieth-century waste land that includes moral decay—within and without the moving train—in terms of environmental degradation along the urban corridors that have grown up along the tracks, deconstructing the monuments of the forefathers:

> monuments, traffic, fields once
> green now the vomit
> of rust, wormy dog-bodies,
> spraycanned annunciations
> of garbage in glory that won't quit;

racial and class segregation,

> Who lives here
> but those you want left behind? The unseen
> cook in tents pitched of clothes
> by track-beds;

and personal alienation,

> Sleepers, celebrants, sink in every seat
> around you, their smells jostling. (193, 194)

Each of the poem's first three sections takes up one of these themes, while the final two struggle to reconcile the speaker with the surrogate father, whose ashes they carry, and with his wife, whose resentments and guilts weigh on them both. The poem recalls Robert Penn Warren's later poetry, such as "Old Nigger on One-Mule Cart Encountered Late at Night When Driving Home from Party in the Back Country" or "Last Night Train," and Warren's effort to come to terms with the self and other, to heal historical rifts both regional and national, cultural and personal.

4

In the 1990s Dave Smith has experienced a number of personal and professional transitions, especially a greater engagement with criticism and editing. His more recent volumes of poetry—*Cuba Nights* (1990) and *Night Pleasures* (1992), the latter another selected poems—seem deliberate attempts to delimit his poetic territory, as even the new settings, stories, and styles recall earlier efforts, as in "Southern Crescent." At the same time, Smith continues to develop as a poet; for example, *Fate's Kite* (1996) is a collection of uneasy "sonnets"—all of thirteen lines containing eleven syllables—and most prove elliptical, enigmatic, and effective. *The Wick of Memory: New and Selected Poems, 1970–2000,* promises another reconfiguration of Smith's expanding canon. Smith's other poems invoking trains include "Lael's Song" (1974), "How to Get to Green Springs" (1976), "Negative: The Little Engine That Could" (1981), "Night of the Chickens, North of Joplin" (1981), "Near the Underground Railroad" (1983), "Rainy Day: Last Run" (1983), "Train to St. Andrews, Scotland" (1995), "The History of the Queen City Hotel" (1996), and "Two Dreams" (1997).

In "Two Dreams" a fitful, dreamlike relation ensues between the speaker and a version of Warren himself. The poem's epigraph, "Some dreams come true, some no," is drawn from Warren's "Red Tail Hawk and Pyre of Youth" (1977), which in turn is dedicated "To Harold Bloom," suggesting both intertextuality and influence. Warren must have appreciated Smith's homage, as he agreed to critique and blurb his new and collected volume of 1985, *The Roundhouse Voices*. For Smith, Warren's hawk, shot and stuffed while a boy, becomes his personal albatross, created by a violation of nature paralleling that of the Ancient Mariner, which Warren will finally escape in the hawklike literary vision of what the bird represents on a naturalistic level.

Smith dreams of his own hunting experience in "Two Dreams," a day of frustration at age sixteen when he dozed, only to awaken unprepared:

> I see my weapon's
> halves in my hands, peaceful, unwed, useless as
> Mother and Father, and I wish I might understand
> mistakes, bad decisions, what makes us so careless.
> (*Wick* 19)

Unmanned, he thinks of his family scattered by the railroads and highways,

> but I can't even say why my family's best vanished,
> climbed down from the railroad's heaving cars
> outside Pittsburgh, followed girls to the green sea,
> then nights dreamed of wheels, orange vats of fire,

as well as a distant figure hunting ahead—perhaps the precursor poet working these same woods (*Wick* 19). Awakening to what may be another dream, the elder poet,

> Whiskey in hand offered, he grins, tells me to row
> across the impenetrable dark toward the sun.
> His face, wrinkled and spotted with starlight, says *Now!*
> (*Wick* 20)

Surely, that starlight shines from a dozen Warren poems as the sacramental whiskey reaffirms the humanity of both poets, older and younger, contemplating their dark and dangerous night voyages.

Reading Dave Smith's poetry and his prose convinces me that he is Warren's literary heir in several senses, the most important of which are the great traditions of Southern poetry and criticism. At present, Smith seems much like Warren, near the same stage in his career, with a history of diverse achievements and varied possibilities for the future. At the new century's start, Dave Smith remains perhaps our most important post-Southern poet, as much for his continuities with the poetic heritage of the Southern Renaissance reaching back to the original Fugitive/Agrarians. As such, he gives us another way to regard post-Southernness, not just in poetry but in other literary genres as well, as we will develop more fully in our concluding chapter.

Chapter Ten

Railroads, Culture, the Southern Renaissance, and Post-Southernism

"So listen," Daddy Hickman said. "Let me tell Revern' Bliss a bit about that woman. A few years back she was supposed to get married. She was going to have a big wedding and everything, but then the fellow who she was supposed to marry was killed when his buggy was struck by the Southern at the crossroads and the poor woman seemed to strip her gears."

Ralph Ellison, *Juneteenth*

1

Juneteenth, Ralph Ellison's long-anticipated second novel, appeared at last in 2000, though it was begun almost a half-century earlier. Therefore, its post-Southern identification proves debatable: is it a modernist work published after its time or a postmodernist text existing in an ironic relation to the traditions of its forbears? The title recalls the late emancipation of Texas blacks long after the close of the Civil War, now an ironic celebration of both the promise and the disappointments of Reconstruction. As Ellison puts it in the book, "*So that was it, the night of the Juneteenth celebration,* his mind went on. *The celebration of a gaudy illusion*" (*Juneteenth* 115, italics in original). Certainly the epigraph above suggests the ironic possibilities for the relation of post-Southern fictions to the monumental figures and texts of the Southern Renaissance, most notably in Flannery O'Connor's invocation of Faulkner's Dixie Limited but also in Ellison's own works. Just as Ellison is not the only post-Southern fictionist, Dave Smith is not our only post-Southern poet to essay railroad imagery and symbolism in the contemporary period, though his dialogic recreation of working-class voices in his poetry serves as an interesting and representative example.

A recent collection of lyric works about tracks and trains, Robert Hedin's *The Great Machines: Poems and Songs of the American Railroad,* presents an impressive selection of serious contemporary poets, including several Southerners in addition to Dave Smith, including James Wright, James Dickey, and Randall Jarrell. Both the variety and the quality of the poetry selected for Hedin's volume—as well as the many works of fiction, nonfiction, and drama by both the popular and serious writers discussed in chapters 1 and 9—show that trains and tracks will remain important cultural markers in Southern cultural and literary history as we enter a new century, much as they were throughout most of the last.

During the twentieth century our railroads peaked in overall cultural importance, declined in the face of competing technologies, and regenerated themselves once more as an essential piece in the American cultural mosaic. Even in the period of their most precipitous industrial decline during the 1960s and 1970s, railroads remained a vital element in our popular and serious culture, as indicated by their persistence at the center of diverse cultural texts including movies and television, country music and rock songs, and stories and poems.

Contemporary writers are further extending the cultural and literary tendencies easily discerned in American modernism between the world wars, a period paralleling the Golden Age of American railroading, as we have seen. This so-called second American Renaissance, like the first flowering of our literature in the nineteenth century, involved diverse elements of our culture, though its most important component may be the Southern Renaissance. The related Harlem Renaissance in African American letters, which began when black Southern writers arrived in Northern settings during the 1920s and 1930s, is represented by Ralph Ellison's *Invisible Man* and his other recreations of the modern Middle Passage by way of the rail routes, replicating the geographical directions and historical purposes of the Underground Railroad.

White authors of the Southern Renaissance focused on the

directions of these great movements in both geographical and historical terms as well. Southern women writers, for all their differences from their male counterparts both black and white, wrought gender-specific changes on these railroad images. Eudora Welty's reminiscence, *One Writer's Beginnings,* affirms the matrix of her narrative art in the railroad journeys of her youth. Her real and recreated railroads, like the legendary "I.C." and "Yellow Dog," in her first novel, *Delta Wedding,* provides a focusing example in chapter 6, also with other women writers like Ellen Glasgow, Caroline Gordon, Katherine Ann Porter, Carson McCullers, and Flannery O'Connor.

The several middle-class, white male writers who grew up in the Golden Age of Southern railroading define our major trope in their "affinity for smoke and fury and thunder and speed" (*Unvanquished* 93). Our examples included Robert Penn Warren's recollected railroads in both poetry (chapter 8) and fiction (chapter 5). Thomas Wolfe's trains, both romantic and realistic, in *Look Homeward, Angel* and later, formed the subject of chapter 3. William Faulkner's cultural reconstruction of Mississippi railroads centers his sagas of autobiographical families in both geographical terms, particularly as demonstrated by *Go Down, Moses* (chapter 4) and in the historical terms of the Sartoris family story (chapter 2).

2

In the present cultural climate, however, the future of Southern railroads may be no more secure than the continued existence of the Southern Renaissance or even of Southern literature as traditionally defined. As we have seen, revisionist critics such as Michael Kreyling, Patricia Yaeger, John Carlos Rowe, Forrest G. Robinson, and others seek cultural reparations for the present from the past in the formulation of revised literary histories, canons, and interpretations. Charges intertwined with gender, race, and class in the South seem to militate against the very existence or continuity of a separate time and place for Southern letters. The cultural construct we call, for want of a another term, the Southern Renaissance ended somewhere in the second half of the twentieth century; some might end it earlier with the Second World War, or the last of Faulkner's major works in 1942, or the first of Robert Penn Warren and Eudora Welty in 1946. More recent writing produced below the Mason-Dixon Line might just be contemporary American literature, or perhaps post-Southern letters, as Michael Kreyling terms it in *Inventing Southern Literature*, following Lewis Simpson, Fred Hobson, and others in combining Southern and postmodern considerations. As Kreyling aptly puts it, "The death of southern literature is no less a crucial trope than its origin" (148).

As we discovered in chapter 1, the origins of the Southern Renaissance, and by extension of Southern literature, reveal a dubious paternity, out of William Faulkner and Thomas Wolfe, by way of several odd Fugitive/Agrarians and Louis Rubin. For the revisionists, the death knell of the Southern Renaissance was sounded by the paradigmatic shifts in the cultural configuration of gender, race, and class in the last quarter of the twentieth century. These changes in interpretation generated new literary histories and canons. We have addressed these charges directly in our discussions of changing orientations in regard to gender, race, and class in the later works of William Faulkner, Thomas Wolfe, and Robert Penn Warren, and indirectly through our readings of intertextual relations between these founding figures and Eudora Welty, Ralph Ellison, and Dave Smith.

Certainly Smith, Ellison, and Welty, perhaps the later Warren and Faulkner, and even the later Wolfe, might be considered post-Southern writers in terms of a questioning, ironic, even parodic relation to the traditional formulations, histories, and canons of Southern culture, Southern literature, and the Southern Renaissance. Other figures invoked by Kreyling for their post-Southern differences seem rooted in the matrix of the traditional canon in their continued use of railroads as subject, image, and symbol. For example, William Styron, praised by Kreyling for his putative separation from Faulkner in *The Confessions of Nat Turner* (1967), replicates the Mississippian's subjects and styles in his treatment of "Southside" Virginia in *Lie Down in Darkness* (1951), which opens with one of the longest literary train journeys since Thomas Wolfe's *Look Homeward, Angel*. Likewise, Walker Percy, invoked by Kreyling for the post-Southernism of *The Moviegoer* (1961), clearly recalls both Faulkner's and Warren's

New Orleans in Binx Boling's ironic narration, and Welty's train rides in his Chicago sales trip aboard the Illinois Central. Finally, Cormac McCarthy's Faulknerian vision of the Tennessee mountains may be more than a bit parodic in his grotesque early novels, but it proves most powerful in the pivotal *Suttree* (1979), his train-haunted homage to Thomas Wolfe's Asheville as well as his own home place of Knoxville.

A few more examples of post-Southern narratives with major railroad sequences by or about women, blacks, and working people include, in chronological order: Harriette Simpson Arnow in *The Dollmaker* (1954), with its wrenching image of little Callie Lou's death at an unprotected rail crossing; John Ehle in *The Road* (1967), with its haunting imagery of the black convict laborers lost to the building of the rail lines across the Appalachians; Albert Murray in *Train Whistle Guitar* (1974), with its early evocation of environmental racism among the blacks living on the wrong side of the L&N tracks in Mobile; Lee Smith in *Oral History* (1983), with its Faulknerian sense of time and place, including a map stitched by the narrow-gauge rail line that decides the contemporary fate of her mountain "holler folks"; Fannie Flagg in *Fried Green Tomatoes at the Whistle Stop Café* (1987), with its alternation of death and redemption on the rail line appropriated by women nurturing the poor outside the Birmingham rail yards during the Depression; and, finally, Bobbie Ann Mason in *Feather Crowns* (1993), with the centrality of the railroad as symbol of change in the lives of farming families in rural western Kentucky at the turn of the twentieth century.

3

William Faulkner's preeminence is challenged by these recent works of women, which seem more indebted to Eudora Welty's pervasive influence (Hobson 9). The revisionist reading of the Southern canon correctly views the secondary role of women in the critical formation of the Southern Renaissance as limiting meaningful dialogue on gender in regional writing and culture (Yaeger 34). Eudora Welty's extensive, important body of work is often posited by revisionist readers, particularly feminists, as a female canon to balance the centrality of texts generated by

Flannery O'Connor's "Dixie Limited" (Yaeger 60). Certainly, Welty seems a worthy matriarch to challenge the doggedly patriarchal conceptions of the Southern Renaissance and to represent the feminine line of modern Southern letters from the mid-century to the present. Interestingly enough for our purposes here, Welty also balances with Faulkner in terms of the imagery and symbolism of tracks and trains.

Railroads pervade her fiction, as we saw in chapter 6, which is focused by her first, best, and most representative novel, *Delta Wedding* (1946). Welty's brilliant memoir, *One Writer's Beginnings,* combines autobiographical reminiscence and literary analysis to demonstrate the sources of her fiction in both everyday life and the life of the mind. The book, her only effort at self-biography, began as a series of three lectures for the American Studies program at Harvard in 1983 and might be considered her own post-Southern commentary on the canon. Entitled "Listening," "Learning to See," and "Finding a Voice," the tripartite structure recreates the pattern of the traditional Bildungsroman or *Kunstlerroman,* as the protagonist develops into the literary artist. *One Writer's Beginnings* proves exceptional as a female variation of a traditionally male genre, one in which the familiar journey/quest motif becomes important in the development of her railroad imagery and symbolism in a decidedly post-Southern sense.

Welty begins the first part of her reminiscence, "Listening," by locating herself in space and time, the house on North Congress Street in Jackson, Mississippi, where she was born in 1909. The tick and gong of the grandfather clock is the first sound she recalls, one "good for a future writer" (3), though her father's love of clocks extends to spatial instruments as well—telescopes, cameras, and gyroscopes fill the house. Christian Welty provided toys of the same sort to "instruct boys and girls (separately)" (3), as Welty puts it. Most important is an electric train: "The engine with its pea-sized working headlight, its line of cars, tracks equipped with switches, semaphores, its station, its bridges, and its tunnel" (5). Also crucial is its distinctive sound: "The elegant rush and click of the train could be heard through the ceiling, running around and around its figure eight" (5). For all her irony, Welty knows that technologies, "but especially the train," represent her father's fundamentally optimistic commitment to the future: "With these gifts he was preparing his children" (5).

In the second part of her reminiscence, "Learning to See," Welty extends the lessons learned from watching the toy train to observing its prototype as she travels with her father by train to visit their relations in Ohio and West Virginia. On these journeys she really learns to both hear and see in narrative terms. "The trips were wholes unto themselves. They were stories. Not only in form, but in their taking on direction, movement, development, change. They changed something in my life: each trip made its particular revelation, though I could not have found words for it" (68). When she did find words to write stories, Welty found her patterns in these journeys, especially in her first novel: "I entered its world—that of the mysterious Yazoo-Mississippi Delta—as a child riding on a train" (68). These quests have their own order, "a timetable not necessarily—perhaps not possibly—chronological. . . . It is the continuous thread of revelation" (68). Thus the railroad timetable becomes an apt trope for the literary text, including *One Writer's Beginnings,* which uses the image to capture time and space on a single page spread out on the reader's knee.

"Finding a Voice," the third part of her reminiscence, opens with an extended description of one of the train trips with her father that focuses our attention on the timetable once more. "I had a window seat. Beside me, my father checked the progress of the train by moving his finger down the timetable and springing open his pocket watch" (73). All the details observed in miniature on the electric train set are here seen for the first time in real life: semaphores, switches, signals; just as important are the developed sounds: whistles, wheels, rail joints. "But my father put it all into the frame of regularity, predictability, that was his fatherly gift in the course of our journey" (73). For her father knows these rail lines well; as a young man he courted Chestina Andrews, Welty's mother, over this same route, traveling from his new job in Jackson. When he could afford it, he made the thousand-mile trip. "The rest of the time—every day, sometimes twice a day—the two of them sent letters back and forth by this same train" (75). So the train becomes the source of other literary texts, ones Welty discovers later stored in an old trunk used to make the summer trips to visit the relations in the North. By the time she can read those texts, Welty discovers her father *"living"* on the page (76, emphasis in original): "They seemed to bare, along with his love, the rest of his life to me" (76).

Finally, these train journeys, in all their realistic and imaginative detail, become quests of self-discovery. Welty's youthful alter ego seems a good deal like one of Thomas Wolfe's fictive protagonists, or one of Robert Penn Warren's poetic personae, viewing a moonlit world from a passing Pullman window, wondering at "what lay beyond, where the path wandered off through the pasture, the red clay road climbed and went over the hill or made a turn and was hidden in the trees, or toward a river whose bridge I could see but whose name I'd never know" (74–75). Like these other modernists who came of age in the golden years of Southern rail travel, Welty is really discovering herself reflected in the pane of Pullman glass. "It was when I came to see it as *I* who was passing that my self-centered childhood was over" (76, emphasis in original).

After her father's early death in the first years of the Depression, Eudora Welty is left to make her journey alone into the world as a young woman. She saves enough from a miscellany of employment in Mississippi to try her hand as a writer in New York City. Once again, however, we hear more of the northbound rail journey than the Northern residence. In another lengthy description of tracks, trains, and stations, Welty skips the great cathedrals of transportation in the metropolis for the gritty Union Stations of Jackson and Meridian in Mississippi. The former is depicted by its final view of a hand-lettered sign on an adjacent wooden building inquiring, "Where Will YOU Spend Eternity?" (95, emphasis in original). The latter is represented by its presiding genius, "the ancient and familiar figure of the black lady" who provided coffee and called the midnight train connections "like words in a church" (94–95).

Fittingly, Welty concludes her narrative with another fictive rail journey, this one from her final novel, *The Optimist's Daughter* (1970), a faintly autobiographical homage to her father, "the train lover" (94), who she recalls through finding his collection of old railway timetables. Welty's reminiscence ends with a quotation from the novel extending over three pages. Af-

ter her father's death, the novel's protagonist recalls riding southward on the Illinois Central and reflecting on the confluence of
the Ohio and the Mississippi as seen from the high bridge at
Cairo, Illinois—an image of the constantly changing yet continu-
ously faithful streams of memory. *One Writer's Beginnings* demonstrates how many of Eudora Welty's memories and how much
of her shaping of them are determined by the train journeys of
her youth, on the same trains that wend their ways into the writ-
ings of William Faulkner, Thomas Wolfe, and Robert Penn Warren. At the same time, her named trains, like the Nashville Rocket
of *Losing Battles,* suggest an ironic attitude toward monumental
male forebears similar to Flannery O'Connor's, one that may be
rediscovered in the fiction of Lee Smith, Alice Walker, Bobbie
Ann Mason, and other post-Southernists—male and female, white
and black, novelists and poets.

4

So we might conclude where we began, with the image of the
modern South's best-known train, the Dixie Limited. This all-
Pullman, extra-fare, express train raced over the Nashville, Chattanooga, and St. Louis Railway's "Dixie Line" between Atlanta
and Chicago, by way of the "Heart of Dixie." Its colorful name
was initiated early in the twentieth century to advertise its essential modernity to the traveling public. The particular incarnation remembered best is a semi-streamlined version powered
by one of the N.C. & St. L.'s powerful J-3 or "Dixie" class, 4-8-4
wheeled, steam locomotives in the era of the Southern Renaissance. The Limited guaranteed to make its trip "on the adver-
tised" overnight schedules, sometimes touching 100 miles an hour
over the "high iron" of the Dixie Line between Nashville and Atlanta (Beebe and Clegg 214–17).

   Of course, this service, limited to those able to pay the extra
fare, attended by white-jacketed blacks, powered by a phallic,
streamlined steam locomotive, and controlled by a male train
crew, also raises interesting complexities of a cultural reading in
terms of class, race, and gender. At once the apogee of high-mod-
ern styling and high-speed power, the Limited was only a version
of the original "iron horse," the steam locomotive, soon to be su-

perannuated by a diesel technology four times as efficient. No wonder Flannery O'Connor could discover no better simile to define the place of William Faulkner in the Southern Renaissance.

Number 576, one of the few extant representatives of the Dixie class locomotives, can be found preserved in Nashville's Centennial Park—not far from either Union Station or, appropriately enough, Vanderbilt University. In stilled power, it appears ready to be fired again, though it will probably continue its present service as a huge plaything for the wonder of current and future children. For those of us old enough to remember, it recalls a once glorious, if limited, existence. As a boy, it was my good fortune to have visited these monsters alive and breathing at trackside, to have climbed into locomotive cabs amidst clanging fire doors, hissing flues, and fluctuating gauges, and to have ridden in the Pullman Standard cars of trains like the Dixie Limited in their last days under steam. These formative experiences instilled my lifelong love of railroads and, after a career-long engagement with Southern literature and culture, perhaps determined the track of the present study.

I trust that I have accomplished at least a portion of what I set out to provide here—a reading of the complex, often ambivalent relation between technology and culture represented by railroads in selected literary texts of the Southern Renaissance. It becomes even more appropriate, as we enter the twenty-first century, that we recall how much the twentieth-century South was shaped by railroads built in the nineteenth century, and how much our future will be determined by the technological and cultural tracks laid down before and after us. In terms of Southern studies, we should remember that, after all, Southern culture does exist, that it produced Southern literature, and that the apogee of these developments was the Southern Renaissance. This cultural and literary development embraces writers as similar yet diverse as William Faulkner, Thomas Wolfe, Robert Penn Warren, Eudora Welty, Ralph Ellison, Dave Smith, and many others both mentioned above or not, or perhaps still to be discovered, as we speed along tracks both practical and mythic, as Allen Tate put it early on, toward our shared, technologically mediated, post-Southern fate.

Works Cited

Aiken, Charles S. "A Geographical Approach to William Faulkner's 'The Bear.'" *Geographical Review* 71 (1981): 446–59.

Ayers, Edward. *The Promise of the New South: Life After Reconstruction.* New York: Oxford Univ. Press, 1992.

Beck, Charlotte. *The Fugitive Legacy.* Baton Rouge: Louisiana State Univ. Press, 2001.

Beebe, Lucius, and Charles Clegg. *The Trains We Rode.* New York: Promontory Press, 1990.

Beja, Maurice. "The Escapes of Time and Memory." In *Thomas Wolfe: Modern Critical Views.* Ed. Harold Bloom. New York: Chelsea House, 1987.

Bloom, Harold. Foreword to *The Collected Poems of Robert Penn Warren.* Ed. John Burt. Baton Rouge: Louisiana State Univ. Press, 1998.

Blotner, Joseph. *Faulkner: A Biography.* New York: Random House, 1974.

———. *Robert Penn Warren: A Biography.* New York: Random House, 1997.

Botkin, B.A., and Alvin F. Harlow, eds. *A Treasury of Railroad Folklore.* New York: Crown Publishers, 1953.

Brooks, Cleanth. "Episode and Anecdote in the Poetry of Robert Penn Warren." In *Community, Religion, and Literature: Essays by Cleanth Brooks.* Columbia: Univ. of Missouri Press, 1995.

Bryant, Joseph. *Twentieth-Century Southern Literature.* Lexington: Univ. Press of Kentucky, 1997.

Bunting, Charles T. "The Interior World: An Interview with Eudora Welty." *Southern Review* 8 (1972): 711–35.

Busby, Mark. *Ralph Ellison.* New York: Twayne, 1991.

Carstens, Hal. *Circus Trains, Trucks, and Models.* Newton, N.J.: Carstens, 1990.

Castner, Charles B., Jr. *The Dixie Line: Nashville, Chattanooga, and St. Louis Railway.* Newton, N.J.: Carstens, 1995.

Cobb, James C. *The Most Southern Place on Earth: The Mississippi Delta and the Roots of Regional Identity.* New York: Oxford Univ. Press, 1992.

Donald, David Herbert. *Look Homeward: A Life of Thomas Wolfe*. New York: Little, Brown, 1987.

Duclos, Donald P. "Colonel Falkner: Prototype and Influence." *Faulkner Journal* 3 (1987): 35–44.

Duvert, Elizabeth. "Faulkner's Map of Time." *Faulkner Journal* 2 (1986): 14–28.

Ellison, Ralph. *Flying Home and Other Stories*. Ed. John F. Callahan. New York: Random House, 1996.

———. *Going to the Territory*. New York: Random House, 1986.

———. *Invisible Man*. New York: Random House, 1952, 1982.

———. *Juneteenth*. Ed. John F. Callahan. New York: Random House, 2000.

———. "A Song of Innocence." *Iowa Review* 1 (1970): 30–40.

Faulkner, William. *Big Woods*. New York: Random House, 1955.

———. *Faulkner at West Point*. Ed. Joseph Fant and Robert Ashley. New York: Random House, 1964.

———. *Flags in the Dust*. Ed. Douglas Day. New York: Random House, 1973.

———. *Go Down, Moses*. New York: Random House, 1942, 1995.

———. *Requiem for a Nun*. New York: Random House, 1951, 1975.

———. *Sanctuary*. New York: Cape and Smith, 1931, Vintage, 1995.

———. *Sartoris*. New York: Random House, 1929, 1975.

———. *The Sound and the Fury*. New York: Random House, 1929, 1959.

———. *The Unvanquished*. New York: Random House, 1938, 1990.

Ferris, William. *Blues from the Delta*. Garden City, N.Y.: Anchor Doubleday, 1978.

Folks, Jeffrey J. *Southern Writers and the Machine: Faulkner to Percy*. New York: Peter Lang, 1993.

Goff, Brian, and S. Lile. "The Tobacco Wars: Evidence of Monopsony or Rent Seeking." *Kentucky Journal of Economics and Business* 15 (1996): 1–22.

Gray, Richard. *The Literature of Memory: Modern Writers of the American South*. Baltimore: Johns Hopkins Univ. Press, 1977.

———. *Southern Aberrations: Writers of the American South and the Problems of Regionalism*. Baton Rouge: Louisiana State Univ. Press, 2000.

Gretlund, Jan N. *Eudora Welty's Aesthetics of Place*. Newark: Univ. of Delaware Press, 1995.

Hansen, Peter A. "Casey Jones: The Brave Engineer." *Trains* 60 (2000): 34–43.

Hardy, John Edward. "Delta Wedding as Region and Symbol." *Southern Review* 60 (1952): 397–417.

Hedin, Robert, ed. *The Great Machines: Poems and Songs of the American Railroad.* Iowa City: Univ. of Iowa Press, 1996.

Hobson, Fred. *The Southern Writer in the Post-Modern World.* Athens: Univ. of Georgia Press, 1991.

Johnson, Charles. Preface to *Juneteenth,* by Ralph Ellison. Ed. John F. Callahan. New York: Random House, 2000.

Jones, J.H. "Penitentiary Reform in Mississippi." *Publications of the Mississippi Historical Society* 6 (1902): 111–28.

Justus, James H. *The Achievement of Robert Penn Warren.* Baton Rouge: Louisiana State Univ. Press, 1981.

Kimball, Sue Laslie. "Thomas Wolfe's Love Affair with Railroads." *West Virginia University Philological Papers* 34 (1988): 74–82.

King, Richard. *A Southern Renaissance: The Cultural Awakening of the American South, 1930–1955.* New York: Oxford Univ. Press, 1980.

Kinnamon, Kenneth. *The Emergence of Richard Wright: A Study in Literature and Society.* Urbana: Univ. of Illinois Press, 1973.

Kreyling, Michael. *Inventing Southern Literature.* Oxford: Univ. Press of Mississippi, 1998.

Ladd, Barbara. "'Coming Through': The Black Initiate in *Delta Wedding.*" *Mississippi Quarterly* 41 (1988): 541–51.

Lemley, James H. *The Gulf, Mobile, and Ohio.* Homewood, Ill.: Irwin, 1953.

Lester, Cheryl. "Racial Awareness and Arrested Development: *The Sound and the Fury* and the Great Migration (1915–1928)." In *The Cambridge Companion to William Faulkner.* Ed. Philip M. Weinstein. Cambridge: Cambridge Univ. Press, 1995: 123–45.

Marrs, Suzanne. "Eudora Welty's Photography: Images into Fiction." In *Critical Essays on Eudora Welty.* Ed. W. Craig Turner and Lee E. Harding. Boston: G.K. Hall, 1989. 280–96.

Marx, Leo. *The Machine in the Garden: Technology and the Pastoral Ideal in America.* New York: Oxford Univ. Press, 1964.

Meredith, William. *The Cheer.* New York: Knopf, 1980.

Millichap, Joseph R. *Robert Penn Warren: A Study of the Short Fiction.* Boston: G.K. Hall, 1992.

Moore, Carol A. "Aunt Studney's Sack." *Southern Review* 16 (1980): 591–96.

Nelson, Scott Reynolds. *Iron Confederacies: Southern Railways, Klan Violence, and Reconstruction.* Chapel Hill: Univ. of North Carolina Press, 1999.

O'Connor, Flannery. "Some Aspects of the Grotesque in Southern Fiction." In *Mystery and Manners.* Ed. Sally and Robert Fitzgerald. New York: Farrar, Straus, and Giroux 1969. 36–50.

Robinson, Forrest G. "A Combat with the Past: Robert Penn Warren on Race and Slavery." *American Literature* 67 (1995): 511–30.

Rowe, John Carlos. "The African-American Voice in Faulkner's *Go Down, Moses.*" In *The Modern American Short Story Sequence: Composite Fictions and Fictive.* Ed. J.G. Kennedy. New York: Cambridge Univ. Press, 1995. 75–97.

Rubin, Louis D., Jr. "The Boll Weevil, the Iron Horse, and the End of the Line: Thoughts on the South." In *A Gallery of Southerners.* Louisiana State Univ. Press, 1979. 197–222.

———. "The Dixie Special: William Faulkner and the Southern Renascence." In *Mockingbird in the Gum Tree: A Literary Gallimaufry.* Louisiana State Univ. Press, 1990: 37–62.

———. *A Memory of Trains.* Columbia: Univ. of South Carolina Press, 2001.

Sartre, Jean-Paul. "Time in Faulkner: *The Sound and the Fury.*" In *William Faulkner: Three Decades of Criticism.* Ed. Frederick J. Hoffman and Olga Vickery. East Lansing: Michigan State Univ. Press, 1960. 225–32.

Shepherd, Allen G. "Robert Penn Warren's 'Prime Leaf' as Prototype of *Night Rider.*" *Studies in Short Fiction* 17 (1970): 343–45.

Simpson, Lewis. *The Brazen Face of History.* Baton Rouge: Louisiana State Univ. Press, 1994.

Singal, Daniel J. *The War Within: Victorian to Modern Thought in the American South, 1918–1945.* Chapel Hill: Univ. of North Carolina Press, 1982.

———. *William Faulkner: The Making of a Modernist.* Chapel Hill: Univ. of North Carolina Press, 1997.

Smith, Dave. *In the House of the Judge.* New York: Harper & Row, 1983.

———. *The Wick of Memory: New and Selected Poems, 1970–2000.* Baton Rouge: Louisiana State Univ. Press, 2000.

Smith, Frank E. *The Yazoo.* Rivers of America series. New York: Rinehart, 1954.

Stover, John F. *American Railroads.* 2nd ed. Chicago: Univ. of Chicago Press, 1997.

———. *The Railroads of the South, 1865–1900.* Chicago: Univ. of Chicago Press, 1955.

Walser, Richard. "Thomas Wolfe's Train as Symbol." *Southern Literary Journal* 21 (1988): 3–14.

Warren, Robert Penn. *All the King's Men.* New York: Harcourt, 1946, 1959.

———. *The Circus in the Attic and Other Stories.* New York: Harcourt, 1947, 1984.

——. *The Collected Poems of Robert Penn Warren.* Ed. John Burt. Baton Rouge: Louisiana State Univ. Press, 1998.

——. *Jefferson Davis Gets His Citizenship Back.* Lexington: Univ. Press of Kentucky, 1980.

——. *Night Rider.* Boston: Houghton Mifflin, 1939, 1959.

——. *A Place to Come To.* New York: Random House, 1977.

——. *Portrait of a Father.* Lexington: Univ. Press of Kentucky, 1988.

Watson, James G. *William Faulkner: Self-Presentation and Performance.* Austin: Univ. of Texas Press, 2000.

Wells, Dean Faulkner. "The Trains Belonged to Everybody: Faulkner as Ghost Writer." *Southern Review* 12 (1976): 864–71.

Welty, Eudora. *Delta Wedding.* New York: Harcourt, 1946.

——. *One Writer's Beginnings.* Cambridge, Mass.: Harvard Univ. Press, 1984.

Weston, Ruth D. *Gothic Traditions and Narrative Techniques in the Fiction of Eudora Welty.* Baton Rouge: Louisiana State Univ. Press, 1994.

——. "Images of the Depression in the Fiction of Eudora Welty." *Southern Quarterly* 32: 80–91.

Williamson, Joel. *William Faulkner and Southern History.* New York: Oxford Univ. Press, 1993.

Wimsatt, Mary Ann. "Religion, Time, and Memory: *The Optimist's Daughter* as Southern Renaissance Fiction." In *The Late Novels of Eudora Welty.* Ed. Jan Nordby Gretlund and Karl Heinz Westorp. Columbia: Univ. of South Carolina Press, 1998. 134–44.

Winn, Thomas A. "*Night Rider* Revisited: An Historical Perspective." *Southern Quarterly* 31 (1993): 68–74.

Wittenberg, Judith Bryant. "*Go Down, Moses* and the Discourse of Environmentalism." In *New Essays on* Go Down, Moses. Ed. Linda Wagner Martin. New York: Cambridge Univ. Press, 1996. 49–71.

Wolfe, Thomas. *The Face of a Nation.* New York: Literary Guild, 1939.

——. *The Hills Beyond.* New York: Harper, 1941, 1955.

——. *The Letters of Thomas Wolfe.* New York: Scribner's, 1956.

——. *Look Homeward, Angel.* New York: Scribner's, 1929, 1957.

——. *The Notebooks of Thomas Wolfe.* Ed. Richard S. Kennedy and Paschal Reeves. 2 vols. Chapel Hill: Univ. of North Carolina Press, 1970.

——. *The Story of a Novel.* New York: Scribner's, 1936.

——. *Of Time and the River.* New York: Scribner's, 1935, 1957.

——. *The Web and the Rock.* New York: Harper, 1939, 1966.

——. *You Can't Go Home Again.* New York: Harper, 1940, 1966.

Yaeger, Patricia. *Dirt and Desire: Reconstructing Southern Women's Writing.* Chicago: Univ. of Chicago Press, 2000.

Index

* 9 7 8 0 8 1 3 1 2 2 3 4 2 *